Other titles in this series:

THE ONE MINUTE MANAGER
Ken Blanchard and Spencer Johnson

PUTTING THE ONE MINUTE MANAGER TO WORK
Ken Blanchard and Robert Lorber

THE ONE MINUTE SALES PERSON
Spencer Johnson

LEADERSHIP AND THE ONE MINUTE MANAGER
Ken Blanchard, Patricia Zigarmi and Drea Zigarmi

THE ONE MINUTE MANAGER MEETS THE MONKEY
Ken Blanchard, William Oncken Jr. and Hal Burrows

THE ONE MINUTE MANAGER BUILDS HIGH PERFORMING TEAMS
Ken Blanchard, Donald Carew and Eunice Parisi-Carew

RAVING FANS!
Ken Blanchard and Sheldon Bowles

GUNG HO!
Ken Blanchard and Sheldon Bowles

BIG BUCKS!
Ken Blanchard and Sheldon Bowles

HIGH FIVE!
Ken Blanchard, Sheldon Bowles, Don Carew and Eunice Parisi-Carew

THE LITTLE BOOK OF COACHING
Ken Blanchard and Don Shula

THE ONE MINUTE APOLOGY
Ken Blanchard and Margret McBride

THE ON-TIME, ON-TARGET MANAGER
Ken Blanchard and Steve Gottry

THE ONE MINUTE GOLFER
Ken Blanchard

leadership by the book

tools to transform your workplace

KEN BLANCHARD
BILL HYBELS
PHIL HODGES

HarperCollins*Publishers*

HarperCollins*Publishers*
77–85 Fulham Palace Road,
Hammersmith, London W6 8JB

www.harpercollins.co.uk

A Paperback Original 2001
7

ISBN 0 00 711453 2

Printed and bound in Great Britain by
Clays Ltd, St Ivs plc

To

all leaders who struggle daily

to produce good results and

bring out the best in themselves and others

Pg-134 Ducks & Eagles

Contents

Introduction

If you're like most leaders in today's complex, fast-paced world, you've sensed a desperate need for a relevant and competent role model of effective leadership. You long for some true standard of perfection and rightness in leadership.

We believe there *is* a perfect practitioner and teacher of effective leadership. That person is Jesus of Nazareth, who embodied the heart and methods of a fully committed and effective servant leader.

People today seeking practical advice on effective leadership rarely give serious consideration to Jesus. This is true of people with different religious beliefs as well as many who call themselves followers of Jesus. For whatever reason, Jesus is not regarded as a relevant model and teacher of how to inspire, direct, and equip people to produce good results.

In this book we invite students of leadership from all faiths, cultures, and experience to take another look at the leadership genius of Jesus. In three years he demonstrated a radical form of servant leadership that created spectacular results with otherwise ordinary people, thereby transforming the course of human history.

By presenting this message of unified moral character, sound method, and consistent behavior, we hope to bring new hope to a world in desperate need of leadership revival.

Leadership by the Book tells a story that portrays three different leaders—at least one of whom is probably much like you—and how together they were able to tap into the leadership principles of Jesus in a practical and effective way.

We recommend, as your approach to this book, that you read through once to follow the story, then again with pen or marker in hand to highlight the major principles and methods. For your assistance, these practical guidelines are summarized in the book's closing pages.

As authors, we bring very different backgrounds to this book. Ken has spent more than thirty years writing and teaching about leadership. Bill, a pastor as well as an author, has focused his energy for more than two decades on building up Willow Creek Community Church in suburban Chicago, and in teaching others what he has learned about leadership along the way. Phil, meanwhile, has been living out his faith in the marketplace as a practicing manager and consultant in the areas of labor relations and human resource management.

While *Leadership by the Book* is a parable about a professor, a minister, and a businessman, it isn't meant to be autobiographical. But it is a story that allows us to share our common commitment to help organizational leaders—whether in business, churches, educational institutions, governmental agencies, the military, or volunteer groups—to create a legacy of significance by implementing the servant leadership values and practices modeled by Jesus.

We hope this book arrives in the nick of time to help you develop servant leadership as your natural, spontaneous response to whatever role you're called to play—so that whether you're making your own decisions or carrying out someone else's, whether you're issuing instructions or obeying orders, whether you're pioneering something new or facilitating someone else's vision, you will do it *to serve* . . . and in the process, produce good results by bringing out the best in yourself and others. God bless you in this endeavor.

Ken Blanchard
Bill Hybels
Phil Hodges
Fall 1999

1
The Heartbreak

When the plane touched down, the Professor awoke from a sound sleep. With all the traveling he did, he counted as one of his blessings that he could sleep anywhere. As the 727 taxied to the gate, the Professor pondered his visit the previous night with Michael.

Michael was considered by many—especially the analysts on Wall Street—to be one of the top managers and business leaders in the country. At one time, the Professor had been proud to consider Michael his best pupil as well as a very good friend. During the three and a half years he had mentored Michael, the Professor and his wife, Allison, had become close friends with Michael and his wife, Carla. Both families lived in the same community just outside of San Diego. They shared common interests, and because their kids were the same age, they often took family vacations together.

The Professor and Michael started to drift apart when Michael accepted a big opportunity in New York. After a few months of fairly regular contact, Michael started to be slow to return calls from the Professor. When they did talk, if the Professor inquired about something Michael was doing or made any suggestions, there would be an awkward silence at the other end of the phone, or Michael would say he had to take another call.

Maybe it was Michael's attraction to fame and fortune or the pressure to succeed, but whatever it was, the Professor's relationship with Michael had slowly faded over the last five years.

Then why last night?

Their reunion had been initiated by Carla. Although he and Michael had lost contact, Carla and Allison had kept in touch over the years. The Professor knew through Allison that Carla was worried about Michael, but he hadn't discovered how out of kilter things were until Carla had called him in tears several weeks earlier.

"I don't even know Michael anymore," Carla wept, "and neither do the kids. All he has time for is work and the next deal. Michael has always worked hard, but he managed to spend time with me and the children. He never does anymore," she said.

"He doesn't seem to be close to or care about anyone at the office, either," Carla continued. "All that counts with him is the bottom line and what the Wall Street analysts think. I'm starting to think I'm living with a stranger.

"Michael used to listen to you," Carla pleaded with the Professor. "Would you talk to him? You're my last resort."

As good luck would have it, Michael and Carla's home north of New York City was less than an hour's drive from where the Professor was due to conduct a leadership seminar in a few weeks. Sensing Carla's desperation and being concerned about Michael, the Professor rearranged his schedule to visit them while he was nearby.

"Michael usually gets home around nine o'clock," Carla said, thrilled to hear the Professor's plan. "I think it would be best if you just surprised him with a visit, saying you were in the area and thought you'd stop by . . ."

As the Professor walked off the plane in San Diego, he was still thinking about last night's visit with Michael. He usually took the shuttle bus home because parking around the airport was expensive and the traffic a real zoo. However, this night, much to his surprise, Allison was at the gate to meet him.

As they hugged, Allison said, "I have some bad news. Michael had a heart attack this afternoon and he's in critical condition."

The Professor felt weak in the knees at the impact of Allison's words. He'd been with Michael less than twenty-four hours earlier.

"Carla called just as I got home from the office," continued Allison. "She sounded numb. It seems that Michael stopped by the health club for a workout and just collapsed on the exercise bike. They called 911 and the paramedics rushed him to the hospital. He's in intensive care. I think we should get on a plane early tomorrow so we can be there to support Carla and pray for Michael."

The Professor nodded in agreement.

This shocking news about Michael quickly brought someone else to the Professor's mind. He turned to Allison and asked if she'd called the Minister.

"Yes, I did," she said. "I knew you would want him to know.

"He'll meet us tomorrow night at the hospital," continued Allison.

"Great," said the Professor. "Thanks for thinking about him."

The Minister, who had worked with the Professor in mentoring Michael years ago, was now living in Dallas on a summer sabbatical leave from his church, engaged in a special assignment at his old divinity school.

As they waited for his luggage, the Professor told Allison about his visit with Michael the previous night. "I arrived at their house before Michael had returned from work," said the Professor. "Carla greeted me with a hug that seemed one part joy at seeing an old friend, and one part relief that help had arrived.

"As we settled down in the den to talk, Carla filled me in on more of the background of Michael's situation. She told me that after Michael's big promotion and their move, he had plunged into his new job with all his characteristic energy and enthusiasm. His work schedule had been horrendous, but Michael's drive to succeed and his natural competitive nature seemed at first to fit well with the new demands.

"At the same time, Carla said, she had been engrossed in getting their two children settled in new schools, as well as in decorating their new home. 'We were so busy that first year,' she recalled, 'and so excited about all the new opportunities opening up for us that we didn't take time to realize what was happening to our private world. It just crept up on us, and we were in deep trouble before we even realized something was wrong.' "

Carla explained how the same gradual erosion seemed to have taken over Michael's spiritual health as well. But she mentioned one ray of hope: Michael had recently told her about meeting a top corporate manager who struck him as a model of efficiency and effectiveness. She was very successful at work but also had time for her family. Everyone admired her—her people, her family, friends, and neighbors. Michael mentioned in passing to Carla that when he asked the woman how she did it, she replied, "I simply work day to day to fulfill the Lord's purpose in my life." Carla was grateful that this woman's words had impressed Michael strongly enough for him to remember and repeat them.

"When Michael arrived home about an hour later," the Professor continued, "he joined us in the den and expressed surprise at seeing me. After about ten minutes of small talk, Carla excused herself, saying she was tired and had an early appointment the next day."

The Professor then related to Allison how at first both he and Michael searched awkwardly for words. It had been so long since they had seen each other face to face. "But eventually we began to reminisce about old times and what we'd learned from each other during our weekly meetings with the Minister.

"As we talked into the night," the Professor told Allison, "I sensed that Michael regretted what had happened to his life. He admitted how the pressure at work had separated him from his people and eroded away his time with Carla and the kids. All his energy was focused on the bottom line and being successful at work, and yet he talked wearily about his loneliness and the choices he'd made the last few years.

"By the end of the evening," the Professor continued as he retrieved his bag, "we'd even made plans to get together again."

Allison sighed. "Carla and I were praying that would happen," she said as they made their way out of the terminal. "And now this!"

* * *

Late that night, back in New York, Michael gradually woke up. His first sensation was of fear and frustration. He recalled the sharp, stabbing pain in his chest and the feeling of heaviness in his arms and legs as he slumped on the exercise bike. He could remember nothing else, but easily imagined what had caused the pain.

Why me? he wondered.

Then the remembrance of his father's untimely death at about this same age brought back the feelings of abandonment and loneliness that had haunted him for years. Was he going to leave Carla and the kids with the same mountain to climb?

Why now—when I was just starting to get some perspective back in my life?

How could he have been so blind to the warning signs? And where was God in all this? Was this some kind of cosmic joke God was playing on him, as his punishment for drifting away?

At least I'm still alive. But he knew he was in trouble. He focused on the sound of the heart monitor and the uncomfortable tubes in his nose. He was vaguely conscious of voices.

Before drifting back to sleep, he called out to God for help with the silent prayer of a frightened child.

2
The Professor

The next morning the Professor and Allison were back at the airport to catch a flight for New York. Their travel would take most of the day, so they had plenty of time for reflection.

As the Professor leaned back in his seat, he began to think about the Minister. He was looking forward to seeing his old friend, and memories of their relationship kept flashing through his mind. He recalled as if it were yesterday his first meeting with the Minister, a meeting triggered by a phone call the Professor made out of frustrations in his career.

When Allison and he first moved to the San Diego area, the Professor had already enjoyed a successful university career. He started as an administrator, but when the dean he worked for urged him to teach a course, the Professor responded with enthusiasm. The experience changed his life. He had taken enough "bad courses" when he was in school and didn't want to teach one himself. And he didn't. The students loved his way of teaching, and he loved doing it. Rather than lecturing the students all the time, the Professor involved them in the learning process through role-play exercises, discussion of cases, and viewing Hollywood movies.

After that initial success in the classroom, the Professor was asked to collaborate on a textbook with the chairman of the management department. He was flattered and enthusiastically accepted the chairman's invitation.

The management textbook that he and the chairman coauthored became a bestseller in its field. With that accomplishment on his record, the Professor quit his administrative job to teach and write full-time.

Success followed success. By the time he was thirty-five, he was a full professor with tenure—a position one colleague described as the best job in the world, where you have all the freedom of an entrepreneur along with the security of a bureaucrat.

Shortly after his promotion to full professor, the Professor took a sabbatical leave. He and Allison and their children moved to the San Diego area for a year. The timing was perfect for Allison. She had just finished her doctorate and was ready to take some time off to decide what she wanted to do next with her professional life.

During that sabbatical year, the Professor and Allison were asked to conduct a number of leadership seminars for various organizations. Several of the corporation presidents with whom they had worked asked, "What are you two going to do at the end of your sabbatical?"

Their response was, "We're going back to the university."

"But if you're hot, you're hot," they countered. "Why don't you start your own business?"

The thought was exciting but challenging. "We'd love to," they said, laughing, "but we have trouble balancing our checkbook. How are we going to start our own business?"

"We'll help," they responded. And they did! As a result, the Professor and Allison decided to stay in San Diego and launch their own training and consulting business. Since Allison was a better manager than the Professor, she took the reins as president of the company. That freed up the Professor to concentrate on the creative writing and product development side of the business.

It was during this period that the Professor's writing career really began to thrive. With the promotional help of a number of his corporate president friends, the Professor coauthored a bestselling book that was widely acknowledged as a major breakthrough in business leadership. That opened the floodgates. He started writing one popular book after another, as well as conducting a highly successful series of training seminars with Allison and some former colleagues and doctoral students. The consulting and training business grew and prospered.

As he reached his mid-forties, the Professor began to wonder what life was all about. *There must be more to it than just writing books and giving lectures,* he thought.

Despite an extremely successful record of bestsellers, the Professor was disillusioned about the lasting impact of his work. In his books, he'd developed a number of popular leadership concepts and methods that were generally accepted as sound and practical. Managers throughout the world espoused them as "best practices." Yet the Professor could name only a few organizations where his ideas were alive and well and consistently being used. He came to believe that people were content merely to talk about good leadership practices rather than actually implement them. He frequently made the statement, "Most organizations spend all their time looking for the next new management concept rather than following up on what everyone just learned."

What especially troubled the Professor was the research indicating that only about 25 percent of managers who attended leadership training courses or seminars ever did anything with what they learned. *What is it,* he wondered, *that keeps leaders from being committed enough to actually use the concepts they're taught?*

The Professor speculated on whether people in other professions might be experiencing this same frustration. Then he got a flash of the obvious. *Ministers,* he thought. *Every Sunday they share great lessons from the Scriptures with their congregations. And yet, how many people in those congregations actually behave any differently during the next week?*

Few, if any, he supposed. *I wonder how ministers deal with this dilemma?*

Giving any serious thought to ministers was something new for the Professor. Although he'd been named after a Presbyterian minister and attended Sunday school regularly throughout his childhood, the Professor had drifted away from religion when he went to college.

When Allison and he decided to get married, his interest in church had perked up again. But it had come to a screeching halt early in their marriage. A young minister who was their friend became a victim of internal politics and was fired by his congregation.The Professor and Allison were shocked by what had happened to their friend. "If that's what church is all about," they decided, "we don't want anything to do with it."

That attitude prevailed for the Professor until he achieved great success with his writing. Often when he would reread one of his books, the Professor could not remember writing parts of it. It was almost as if the books had "written him." Rather than getting a big head from his success, he began wondering what was going on.

That's when he started looking at his own spirituality and relationship to God. The Professor's spiritual renewal had reawakened Allison's interest in her faith, and together, with the help of some caring friends, they had been on a gratifying spiritual journey for the last decade. They hadn't joined a church, however, because they couldn't find a minister who excited and challenged them, and they were distracted by the squabbling between different denominations.

About the time the Professor was having serious concerns about the lack of impact of his work, he and Allison heard about a church on the other side of town that was said to have the fastest-growing congregation in the region. They had considered attending a service there some Sunday to see if it might have a minister they liked, and a church school that could provide spiritual growth for their kids.

When the Professor realized that ministers might share his concern about impact, he wondered if the pastor of this growing church would have some answers. He decided to give him a call and find out.

After the Professor introduced himself on the phone he was surprised to learn that the Minister had heard of his work. "I've never read any of your books," he said, "but I know some people who swear by you."

"That's what I would like to talk to you about," said the Professor. "I think what I teach is good and can make a difference in how effective leaders are and how well their organizations run. Based on the number of books I've sold and the popularity of my seminars, plenty of people agree with me. But the troubling thing is that their actual practice of these principles on a day-to-day basis is minimal. I don't understand why. I figured maybe you've had a similar experience."

"You mean," said the Minister, laughing, "there might be a disconnect between what I preach on Sunday and how people in the congregation behave."

"Exactly," replied the Professor. "How do you explain that—and what, if anything, do you try to do about it?"

"By all means, let's talk," said the Minister. "How about tomorrow morning at ten in my office?"

Memories of their friendship that began with that first phone call filled the Professor's mind as the plane that carried him and Allison landed in New York. By the time they picked up their luggage, it was after 5:00 P.M., so they decided to go directly to the hospital. "That's where Carla will be," Allison said, and they wanted to be there to give her as much support as possible.

During the taxi ride to the hospital, the Professor offered a silent prayer for Michael's recovery. Then the question occurred to him: *If my prayer is answered and Michael fully recovers, what should I say to him at this point in his life?*

3

Michael

When Allison called the Minister and told him of Michael's heart attack, he and his wife, Peggy, immediately began to pray for his recovery. They also prayed that somehow through this crisis Michael's faith in God might be restored and that Carla would be sustained by her faith during the ordeal.

As the Professor and Allison were flying from the West Coast, the Minister was boarding a plane in Dallas to join them in New York. As the plane took off, the Minister's thoughts soon went back to the day he first met Michael.

They had met on the golf course, where they found themselves paired at a local charity tournament. It turned out they both shared a lifelong love for the great game. This was a legacy that both their fathers had left with them. Michael's father had taught him to hold a club when he was only four years old, while the Minister's dad had done the same for him when he was seven.

The Minister had told Michael he still enjoyed playing golf with his dad more than with anyone else. While they both could be competitive when the occasion presented it, he said, the truth was that they really enjoyed spending time with each other no matter who won or lost.

For Michael, however, playing with his father was no longer an option. He had lost his dad to a sudden heart attack when he was seventeen. But the Minister remembered how Michael's eyes had lit up as he described the competitive battles he and his father had enjoyed before that. He recalled beating his dad for the first time when he was thirteen. Such a victory wasn't a part of his father's child-rearing plans. From then on his dad's competitive spirit was always ignited whenever he and Michael stepped to the first tee.

As the Minister matched Michael shot for shot on the first several holes of their tournament round, they found they enjoyed each other's company. Michael even felt relaxed enough to admit being initially disappointed to be paired with a "man of the cloth." He had hoped to make a new business contact or two by the end of the round. Instead, the two men had planted the seeds of a new friendship. This was particularly meaningful to the Minister when he learned that Michael and his family had recently visited his church.

Later, when the Minister and Peggy got to know Michael and Carla, she explained how they first started attending his church.

While Carla's faith was central to her own life, she had to admit that Michael did not have a very active spiritual life. He'd been willing to stand up and proclaim his faith for the baptism of each of their children, but it took a back seat to the day-to-day struggles of his business life.

She related how Michael had been the epitome of a modern success story. His intelligence, magnetic personality, and competitive drive had carried him through a string of hard-earned achievements, first as a high school and college quarterback, then as an entrepreneur in the fast-paced facilities management business. He drove himself and those around him with a sense of urgency that kept his daily and yearly calendar filled with meetings, phone calls, faxes, e-mails, and travel. The one thing that made this bearable to Carla was that Michael was willing to shut the motor down for important occasions with the kids and would take time to go on periodic family vacations when she insisted.

When they first moved to the community, Carla had insisted that "for the children's sake," they find a church. Michael agreed to shop around for a church until they found one that fit his way of life. After several attempts they finally found one that fit the bill. It was close to home, and the parking lot was never full, which accommodated both their late arrivals and a quick departure if Michael had a plane to catch. The people were well dressed and seemingly successful. Michael had, in fact, made a few good business contacts with members of that congregation. The music was pleasant, and the sermons short and usually entertaining enough to hold his attention without making him too uncomfortable. By the time he and Carla had retrieved the kids from Sunday school and were driving out of the church parking lot, Michael had mentally checked off the experience as a "completed item" in his day planner and was thinking about the business of Monday.

This pattern continued for a number of years. Michael seemed satisfied with remaining in a state of arrested spiritual development while he concentrated on the practical business of getting to the top.

Carla, on the other hand, became increasingly uncomfortable with their weekly Sunday trip to church. For one thing, she felt that something was missing in the pastor's messages, which usually dealt with major social issues of the day. God was mentioned in only a remote way, and Jesus was portrayed as a mystical figure about whom controversy still raged. The Bible was referred to, but copies were not visible—except for the large ornamental version displayed on the altar. She couldn't quite put her finger on what was wrong, but Carla knew there must be something more to a religious experience than what she and Michael—and most importantly, her children—were experiencing.

This became a topic of discussion with one of her friends at her daughter's play group. The friend told Carla about a new church that she was attending. She related that it offered great Sunday school programs for kids and had a dynamic pastor who had really challenged her and her husband to see and experience their faith in a new light.

Cashing in a few chips with Michael (who had recently forgotten their anniversary while on a business trip) Carla persuaded him to go with her to the Minister's church. By the time they found a parking spot in the crowded lot and deposited the kids in a Sunday school class, the service had already begun. Taking some seats in the back row of the gymnasium that the congregation was using while the new church was being finished, Michael and Carla settled in to listen to the pastor's message.

As the service proceeded, Carla became aware of a strange rustling sound that punctuated the Minister's sermon. When she finally identified the source, she was amazed. It was the turning in unison of pages of hundreds of Bibles that the congregation was using to follow along with the Minister's continuing references to specific passages of Scripture. Carla had never been in a church where this occurred, and she found the practice fascinating. (Michael's own Bible—a long-ago gift from a favorite aunt—was neatly tucked away in mint condition in a bookcase down in their basement.)

When the kids came out of Sunday school beaming with excitement because of some new friends they had made, the deal was sealed.

"And so," Carla told the Minister and Peggy, "that's why we quietly left our old church and started attending yours."

Michael confessed to the Minister at one of their early meetings that at first he still considered his church attendance as part of the ticket to keep Carla happy during the frequent seventy-hour weeks he put in to piece together his latest business venture. But over time he'd begun to admire the Minister's obvious preaching talents and deep knowledge of the Bible. This motivated Michael to want to know more about the life and teachings of Jesus. He even purchased a New Testament Bible Study on tape that he started to listen to while he was exercising.

As a result of their growing friendship, Michael and the Minister began to meet occasionally for lunch. They found that they always had much to talk about. Michael was continually amazed and excited as the Minister helped him connect the day-to-day struggles that Jesus faced in leading his disciples with his own struggles at the office.

With these thoughts racing through his mind as he flew toward New York, the Minister found himself longing to talk with Michael again.

4

The Minister

The Minister's thoughts during the flight ran to his good friend the Professor as well. It was while he was getting to know Michael that the Minister first encountered the Professor through a phone call. When the Professor sounded frustrated about the impact of his work, the Minister could easily relate—he, too, had experienced some frustrations during his own career.

As a new seminary graduate, the Minister had served as an associate pastor in an old, established parish with beautiful buildings, a well-to-do congregation, and an active social agenda. His duties were quickly defined by the existing traditions imposed by a strong council of lay members whose families had attended the church for three and four generations. The senior pastor, while kind to his new associate and interested in some of his innovative ideas, had become a reluctant but weary upholder of the status quo.

After a few years of growing frustration with the slow pace and resistance to change, the young Minister began thinking of leaving the ministry for a more energizing and rewarding occupation. At this low point in his career he was contacted by one of his former seminary professors and told about a fledgling new church that was looking for a pastor. The money was meager, and the congregation was meeting only in a high school gymnasium. "But there are some very excited people involved who are looking for a leader," he was told, "and you might be just the right man for the job."

The young Minister had recently married Peggy, his high school sweetheart, so the prospect of poverty-level wages wasn't attractive. However, there was something about the challenge and opportunity of getting in on the ground floor, before everything was set in concrete, that had a magnetic pull to it.

After talking it over with his wife and spending a lot of time on his knees in prayer for guidance, the Minister agreed to be a candidate for the new job. Three months later he said goodbye to the somewhat reassuring century-old buildings and traditional ways of his former assignment and began the daunting effort of shepherding his new flock. The lack of focus, strategy, and resources in the new church quickly engaged all his energies.

During the initial phase, the Minister found that he'd been well prepared at the seminary to answer probing and challenging questions about the Bible and the life of Jesus from a theological standpoint. He also discovered he had a gift for preaching that hadn't been fully utilized in his former assignment. He loved the time he spent preparing his sermons and was pleased, although somewhat surprised, by the very positive response to them from the congregation. Attendance grew steadily, and financial support for the church increased enough to allow him a modest but acceptable lifestyle. He was very busy but also very excited in his new position. Best of all, he regained much of his enthusiasm for his calling to the ministry.

By working long hours and by taking only a few days off, the Minister was able to do a good job guiding the growing complexities of his parish. He made almost all the day-to-day decisions for operating the church because, with the exception of his secretary, his only help came from volunteers from the congregation. Although he had only one vote on the church council, he usually had enough influence to swing a majority his way.

As the years went by and the church continued to grow, the Minister became more and more aware that the strain of being a one-man show was taking a toll on his effectiveness.

Despite convincing the board to hire some additional staff, he still found himself answering most of the questions and spending far too much of his time smoothing ruffled feathers and straightening out messes that his staff and volunteers had made. Having never been formally trained in leadership, he vacillated between being heavy-handed with those under his leadership and allowing them to find their own way with no direction from him.

Even with these managerial shortcomings, the congregation raved about his sermons and attendance continued to grow—creating an even larger workload. He was quickly becoming a victim of his own success.

Over time the Minister came to realize that a "day of reckoning" was on the horizon. He was enough of a leader to predict that the church could not continue to add hundreds of people to its weekly services—and truly serve them well—without developing an infrastructure that could assimilate and equip people. This became a frequent topic of his thoughts and progress.

That's why the Minister sensed that it was no accident that the Professor's phone call came when it did. He needed the Professor as much as the Professor seemed to need him.

As his plane touched down in New York, the Minister's mind turned to the question of how he, Allison, and the Professor could best serve Michael and Carla in their time of crisis. He thought how good it would be to once again join the Professor at Michael's side.

5

The Commissioning

When the Minister arrived at the hospital, the Professor and Allison were already there with Carla. Her face showed the severe strain of her ordeal, but her eyes brightened as the Minister walked in.

"I'm so grateful you've come," she said. "Grateful to all of you."

Carla excused herself momentarily to place a phone call to her sister, who was looking after Michael and Carla's two children during the crisis. Meanwhile, the Minister greeted Allison and the Professor, who summarized the meager information available on Michael's condition. "Although he's regained consciousness, Carla is only allowed to go to the intensive care unit and hold Michael's hand every once in a while," the Professor said. "He's got the best doctors, and they seem to be doing all they can, but his situation is still dangerous."

When Carla rejoined them, they found an empty waiting room just a few paces down the hall from where Michael was being carefully monitored and sat down together. Despite her exhaustion, Carla was eager to talk. She turned first to the Professor.

"I didn't know how late you and Michael stayed up talking the other night, because I was sound asleep when he came to bed. But apparently he hardly slept at all. He woke me early the next morning to say we needed to talk. I could sense in his manner that this was something important, so I went to the kitchen to brew a pot of coffee and to call and cancel a morning appointment I'd scheduled.

"At the breakfast table he immediately began telling me about your conversation, and the thoughts it had stirred in his mind.

"I could hardly believe it," Carla continued. "He was opening his heart to me more than he had in a long, long time. At one point he squeezed my hand, and I saw tears in his eyes. He said, 'Carla, I'm afraid I'm losing touch with my soul.' " Carla shook her head, still amazed at Michael's confession.

"What an answer to our prayers!" the Professor said. "And yet I'm surprised Michael responded so quickly to our discussion."

"It sure surprised me," said Carla. "In fact, Michael spoke at length about wanting to get his priorities back in order and to be a more sensitive and caring person at home. He kept talking about the need to rekindle his servant heart and bemoaned the fact that he'd stopped looking to Jesus as his model for effective leadership. He admitted that once his heart had hardened at work, it affected his relationships at home.

"I can't remember how long it's been since I've heard him discuss things in this way. It was as if he'd just rediscovered all you both taught him. I was so glad—and so proud of him."

Carla was now quietly shedding tears. Allison reached out to put her arm around her friend's shoulders.

The Professor shook his head. "It's so sad that this had to happen just as Michael was at the point of a major turnaround. The timing couldn't have been worse."

"Perhaps," said Allison as she held Carla's hand. "But I believe there are no accidents in life. And you know what? My faith tells me Michael's going to be okay. If that's so, as painful as this is, it might be the best thing that could have happened."

Wiping the tears from her eyes, Carla looked hopefully at the Minister and the Professor. "If the Lord is willing to restore Michael's health and give him another chance," she said, "he's going to need your help in facing the future. I think that's why God has brought you here now—so you can begin planning how to help him. You both are truly faithful friends, and I know you've come here to support me as well as Michael. So I want you to know that the support and effort that would mean the most to me now is knowing you're making plans for how to keep Michael on track when he recovers."

Both men sat momentarily speechless as they absorbed the meaning of Carla's words. Just then Michael's doctor approached and asked to talk to Carla alone. When she returned minutes later, Carla's face showed a slight sense of released tension. She told her friends that "Michael's condition has somewhat stabilized, but the doctor wants to keep him isolated in intensive care until further notice."

Allison suggested that Carla go home to get some rest, and volunteered to go with her to help in whatever way she could. Carla agreed. But before the women left, the Minister led the four in prayer, turning Michael's healing over to the Lord.

When the Professor and the Minister were alone, they sat down in the small waiting room. For a moment they simply gazed silently at each other with the same questioning look on their faces.

"Sounds as if we've been commissioned," the Professor said.

The Minister nodded in agreement.

6

Effective Leadership Starts on the Inside

The hospital corridors around them grew increasingly quiet with each passing moment as the Professor and the Minister weighed the challenge that Carla had left with them. One thing became clear—they needed a plan, and that would take time. So they decided to continue their conversation into the night.

Occasionally a doctor or nurse would emerge through the nearby doors leading from Michael's intensive care unit, but there was no change in his condition to report. As the night wore on, the Professor and the Minister paused from time to time to pray for Michael, then resumed their discussion about how best to respond to Carla's request. They kept coming back to the strong and familiar foundations of what they both had learned over the years.

"From my discussion with him I sensed that Michael had lost track of the internal heart aspect of leadership and was becoming increasingly frustrated with what was happening to his life," said the Minister.

"That was the same aspect of leadership that I was missing when we first spoke," said the Professor. Then a smile came over his face. "I'll never forget how your opening remark shocked me when I acknowledged my frustration with the application and use of my teachings. You said I was looking in the wrong place."

"You were looking on the outside," recalled the Minister. "You were trying to change people's outward behavior. But I'd come to realize that lasting change in people is an inside job."

With that, the two men reviewed the essential points they had talked about in that first conversation years before in the Minister's office.

* * *

"An inside job?" the Professor had asked that morning.

"It's about the heart," explained the Minister.

"So just changing someone's thinking isn't enough?"

"No," said the Minister, "but it's important. The old saying that 'As a man thinks, so he becomes' is still true. But real change in behavior eventually requires a transformation of the heart. That's where the core of who you are resides."

"I certainly haven't zeroed in on that dimension of leadership," said the Professor. "I've been concentrating on leader behavior and methods. But I see your point: I have been trying to change people from the outside."

"I used to do the same thing," responded the Minister. "I focused a lot of energy on teaching the Ten Commandments and the Golden Rule, and telling people how they should behave."

"Was that wrong?" asked the Professor.

"Not necessarily," said the Minister. "Maybe just ineffective. The more I study the Bible and particularly the life and teachings of Jesus, the more I realize that Jesus' message is not just for the mind. It's directed at the heart. It's a real *heart attack.* The underlying message in all his teachings is about character change. Jesus is interested in us becoming different people, not just in our acting differently.

"For instance, rather than asking us just to do kind things, he wants each of us to *become* a kind person. When that happens, *everything* we do will be stamped with kindness even when we must disagree with someone or discipline them. He's telling us to be kind all the time, not just when it suits us."

The Professor mulled over that perspective. "So you might say Jesus doesn't want us just to act honestly because it's the thing to do; he wants us to be honest people at the core of our being. Then honesty will be our automatic response in everything we do."

"Right!" said the Minister. "Jesus hasn't given us detailed instructions on how to handle every situation. There's no set of rules or regulations that automatically tell us what to do. The weakness of rules is that people can always find a way to live comfortably within the letter of the law without it affecting their hearts or character."

"We certainly see that often enough with political leaders and even business leaders," said the Professor. "They seem to adapt any rule or law to fit their own needs or drives. They talk a good game, but you wonder about their motives. Tell me more about the character aspect of leadership."

"I believe there are two kinds of leaders: those who are *leaders first* and those who are *servants first,*" said the Minister.

"How would you describe someone who's a leader first?" asked the Professor.

"People who are *leaders first* are too often those who naturally try to control, to make decisions, to give orders. They're 'driven' to lead—they want to be in charge. And they're possessive about their leadership position—they think they own it. They don't like feedback because they see it as threatening their position, the one thing they most want to hold on to."

"And what about leaders who are servants first?" inquired the Professor.

"Leaders who are *servants first* will assume leadership only if they see it as the best way they can serve. They're 'called' to lead, rather than driven, because they naturally want to be helpful. They aren't possessive about their leadership position—they view it as an act of stewardship rather than ownership. If someone else on the scene is a better leader, they're willing to partner with that person or even step aside and find another role for themselves where they can better serve. They don't have the need to hold on to a leader's role or position if it doesn't make sense from the perspective of service.

"And they love feedback, because they see it as helping them serve better. They truly have servant hearts."

"So their focus is to serve the cause, not to enhance their own positions," commented the Professor.

"Absolutely. And they freely follow their natural motivation—which is to serve—in whatever way is appropriate for the situation: as a leader, as a follower, or as a teammate."

"People who are servant-hearted leaders sound like they're special people," said the Professor. "How do you become like that?"

"Since we're talking about character," responded the Minister, "what you're really asking is, How do you get it?"

"Tell me more," said the Professor.

"To get something, you have to go to the right source," said the Minister. "And there's no better source than Jesus. He exemplified the fully committed servant leader and made 'getting it' accessible to those who decided to follow him.

"On one occasion, he sent an especially clear message about the essence of what kind of leaders his followers were to be. James and John had been vying for a special leadership relationship among his disciples. Jesus used that opportunity to teach something to all twelve men on his team. He first pointed out the overbearing way that ungodly rulers in this world exercised authority over others.

"Then he said, '*Not so with you.* Instead, whoever wants to become great among you must be your servant, and whoever wants to be first must be slave to all.' To further emphasize the point, he immediately mentioned his own example—that he'd come to earth not to be served, but to serve.

"He was mandating a form of leadership that's radically different from the model we're usually most familiar with," continued the Minister. "He showed us that true leadership starts on the inside with a servant heart, then moves outward to serve others. Jesus isn't interested in having us fill a certain quota of servanthood requirements, but in having us develop a servant heart. Then everything we do will be to serve others and the highest good."

"So what you're saying is that character in the form of a servant heart precedes the use of effective leadership methods," said the Professor. "Jesus gives us big-picture guidance about servant leadership so we can apply these general lessons as creatively and honestly as we can in everyday life. Life's not about living with a rigid set of laws, but living in harmony with a servant heart."

"You're hearing me loud and clear," said the Minister. "Jesus was a servant leader who led by example. He wants us to apply his example as a practical and effective way to lead in our daily lives."

"That's going to require many people to think about Jesus and leadership in a new way, isn't it?" asked the Professor.

"Yes," said the Minister. "Some people view him as just a good man, others as a prophet, and true believers see him as the savior of their souls. And yet, although he's universally admired, few people, even his followers, think of him as a relevant leadership model and teacher for their daily lives. Nothing could be further from the truth. As recorded in the Bible, Jesus intends for all his followers to become his students for all aspects of life. He taught us that his example was our guide for having an abundant and meaningful life *now,* and not just in the hereafter."

"When I think about what that means for leaders who are followers of Jesus," said the Professor, "it strikes me that they have a vital role in 'walking their talk' and modeling behaviors he would value."

"That's true," said the Minister. "But remember, the key thing is that the process starts on the inside with who they are—their character—and not by teaching people specific behaviors or methods separated from the motives of their heart."

* * *

That had been the essence of the first discussion the Professor and the Minister had had together, which they now recalled as they talked in the hospital waiting room. "It's helpful to review all this again," said the Professor.

"Although I could tell you were on overload that morning in my office," said the Minister, laughing. "You needed to take some time to think about what I said."

"And that's exactly what I did," said the Professor.

7
Iron Sharpens Iron

"My mind was racing a mile a minute when I left your office that day," the Professor continued, "so I went for a walk on the beach. I kept on hearing your words, *You've been focusing on the wrong area.* That troubled me. How did I get so off-base?

"I knew it was true that I'd been focusing on how leaders should behave rather than on developing sound intentions or character. And as I thought about it there on the beach, I remembered exactly when my focus on methods began.

"When I first entered the management field, no one was studying much about character. Instead the focus was on behavior, particularly leader behavior. Most of the revered leadership theorists contended that there was one 'best' leadership style. This style was usually referred to as a 'team' or 'participative-supportive' style. But when my department chairman and I began writing our textbook, that philosophy didn't make sense to us. We believed that a participative-supportive style could be a good approach in some situations, but a disaster in others.

"I made this point one day in a class I was teaching. I began by asking, 'What would happen if you were the teacher here, and this classroom burst into flames? Would you ask everyone to break into small groups to discuss the best way out of the room, then have each group choose a spokesperson to make a report so the whole group could come to consensus on the best course of action?'

"Of course, everyone in the class agreed that this wasn't the best approach. In a situation like that, someone has to take charge.

"So in the textbook we were writing, my department chairman and I showed the shortcomings of a participative-supportive leadership style and advocated a situational approach to effective leadership. We also highlighted what leaders should do in a variety of different situations, from simple everyday problems to highly complex ones. We developed all kinds of effective methods to help managers lead and motivate people.

"These methods were widely praised and studied by other professionals, who found them highly effective. That's why I couldn't understand why, after training, so few people or organizations were using our methods in their day-to-day management practices. It was a hard pill to swallow.

"As I walked on the beach," continued the Professor, "I realized that at least I wasn't the Lone Ranger. After all, you'd already admitted having the same problem.

"Then I thought about what you'd said about the 'inside job' that's required in effective leadership. Several examples came to mind.

"I'd recently had lunch with a top fitness guru, and I had said to him, 'Be honest with me. Of all the people who come to your fitness center for a diagnosis and prescription session, how many are in any better shape one year later?'

"He told me, 'If I'm really optimistic, I'd say ten to fifteen percent.'

"After our initial discussion," the Professor told the Minister, "it seems obvious that unless there's a way to transform people so they see themselves as healthy people, teaching them new exercise plans or diets is a waste of time.

"Then I recalled being asked by a nutrition expert, 'Why do you eat?' I had all kinds of reasons for eating, whether or not it was mealtime. When I grew up, we ate when we were happy about something, or when we were sad, or anxious, or grateful. . . . Whatever happened, my mother would always say, 'Let's eat.'

"And yet this health expert said that when he asked the same question of naturally thin people—folks who never had a weight problem—they had trouble understanding the question. After all, to them, the answer was so obvious. They didn't eat unless they were hungry. In other words, in their hearts they were 'thin people.'

"Then another example came to mind. I was having dinner one night with one of my oldest and dearest friends. He's in the hotel business, and has helped create more five-star properties than anyone else in the industry. While we were eating, my friend noticed people waiting to be seated, and no one on the staff seemed to be taking care of them. Suddenly he jumped to his feet, approached the waiting people, and began to seat them. When he came back to the table, I asked, 'What were you doing? This isn't even one of your restaurants.'

"My friend said, 'I just couldn't stand seeing guests waiting there and no one helping them. If I hadn't done something, it would have bothered me all night.'

"I realized that his actions were not the result of a learned method as much as a reflection of who he was—a servant at his core when it comes to treating people as guests.

"As I walked on the beach, I began recognizing the strong possibility that the methods I'd been teaching, if they were compatible with Jesus' leadership behavior, could be put to the best long-term use when combined with a servant heart. All this thinking motivated me to learn more about what people with 'servant hearts' are like. That's why I called you to set up another meeting."

The Minister nodded his understanding, then said, "And while you were reflecting on the importance of changing people on the inside, I was reading the books and materials you'd given me, and was reflecting on effective behaviors on the outside. As you remember, I was intrigued by what I read. I found that you had developed some sound leadership concepts and methods that addressed many of the leadership issues I was struggling with in the church. What was really fascinating was to realize that Jesus used these methods in leading his disciples."

"So my colleagues and I didn't invent these concepts," said the Professor with a smile, "we just rediscovered them."

"Right you are," said the Minister.

"I was surprised you never learned any of that at divinity school," said the Professor.

"But we didn't," said the Minister. "We were steeped in the gospel and developing a servant heart, but hadn't learned a thing about leading a growing church, motivating a staff, or enlisting the efforts of a volunteer army. A lot of my leadership, although well-intentioned, was being done by sheer intuition—trial and error. And this approach was getting less effective as our church continued to grow. I needed help. The timing of your second call couldn't have been better."

"I'm glad," said the Professor. "Did anything else catch your fancy while you were reading my material?"

"Yes," said the Minister. "Your writings convinced me that for someone to be an effective servant leader, that person must be able to utilize a servant-leader approach in three domains: intellectual, emotional, and behavioral."

"In other words," the Professor observed, "the head, the heart, and the hands must all be working in harmony."

"Yes," said the Minister. "None of them can stand alone. The head by itself is insufficient, because merely believing in the concept doesn't make a person a servant leader."

"I certainly learned that truth!" said the Professor.

"And I recognized that even when the head and the hands work together—believing and behaving as a servant leader—that didn't necessarily cut it, because some leaders view service as a means to an ego-driven end. They haven't progressed beyond the 'status syndrome.' Eventually, they no longer serve people, but have other people serve them."

"In other words, what they're missing is a servant heart," said the Professor.

"Right," said the Minister. "I also realized that even if you have a servant heart, you can have some problems. That's when I experienced my big 'aha!' from reading your material. Leaders with a servant heart can attempt all kinds of servant leadership activities without being effective. I knew I'd been there, and so had many of my pastor friends. We were using ineffective methods or were lacking leadership skills. Our problem was with our hands—our behavior."

"That's exactly what happens all the time in the marketplace," said the Professor. "Leaders often just don't know how to develop people, and they end up doing all the work themselves. In addition to burning themselves out, their people remain dependent on them and underdeveloped."

"It is possible," the Minister suggested, "that they don't even realize their leadership behavior isn't aligned with their beliefs. They may have good motives and intentions, but lack effective leadership methods. That's where I saw that your focus on sound methods could be of great help. In my ministry I began to anticipate ways I could take my good intentions and put them into more effective action.

"And I developed the hope," added the Minister, "that once ministry leaders with a servant heart learned your leadership concepts and their motives were aligned with true intentions to serve, those concepts could become internalized and part of who they are. I wanted to learn more. That's why I was excited when you called about meeting again."

"I guess we both believed that one plus one could be greater than two," said the Professor.

8

Synergy

"That's what I was counting on when I first got the idea of us both helping Michael," said the Minister.

Their discussion then turned to the circumstances that prompted their deeper involvement in Michael's life. The Minister recalled the occasional lunch meetings he and Michael had after their first golf game. "One was scheduled shortly after you and I had met, and I'd started to read your writings on leadership methods. I was excited to share them with Michael and tell him what I'd learned.

"Michael listened intently," said the Minister, "especially when I concluded that effective leadership involves both character and methods. I remember our conversation as if it were yesterday."

* * *

"I'm glad to hear you've been doing a lot of thinking about leadership lately," said Michael. "I've just been given a real leadership challenge."

"Tell me all about it," said the Minister.

"I've just been asked to take over the Baxter Center and see if I can turn that operation around."

"The old Baxter Center?" asked the Minister.

"That's it," said Michael. "As you know, it includes the Baxter Hotel, plus a number of restaurants and shops and a health club. And your use of the word 'old' is right on, in more ways than one."

"People have told me the hotel once carried a five-star rating, and the entire Center was considered a gem in our town," the Minister said.

"That was after Malcolm Baxter first developed the Center," Michael said. "Unfortunately, when Malcolm died, things began to go downhill fast. His family fought over control of his estate, and no one seemed to have Malcolm's leadership abilities. I met with the family for breakfast this morning and they want me to take over as president and COO of the operation. They realize that the Baxter Center is their main financial asset, and that they don't have the skills to revitalize its old quality."

"It sounds like an exciting opportunity for you, Michael."

"Exciting—and a little scary," Michael replied.

"How so?"

"Well, it's the biggest project I've undertaken, and the condition of the organization is a real mess," said Michael. "There's a lot of bitterness and mistrust. Making this project successful will take everything I have."

"That leads me to think," said the Minister, "that the leadership principles that I have been talking to you about may be more valuable to you now than ever."

"They sound interesting," Michael admitted, "and having Jesus as a leadership model is an intriguing idea, as we've talked about before. But to be honest with you, what does Jesus know about running a business like the Baxter Center?"

"You sound like Simon Peter." The Minister smiled.

"How's that?"

"Open your Bible to Luke 5," said the Minister, grateful that after a few luncheons with Michael, he had persuaded him to bring his Bible along. They read together:

> "One day as Jesus was standing by the Lake of Gennesaret, with the people crowding around him and listening to the word of God, he saw at the water's edge two boats, left there by the fishermen, who were washing their nets. He got into one of the boats, the one belonging to Simon, and asked him to put out a little from shore. Then he sat down and taught the people from the boat.
>
> "When he'd finished speaking, he said to Simon, 'Put out into deep water, and let down the nets for a catch.'
>
> "Simon answered, 'Master, we've worked hard all night and haven't caught anything. But because you say so, I will let down the nets.' "

The Minister looked up from the text and asked, "Can you imagine what Peter was thinking at this point in the story?"

"I can just hear Simon thinking, 'Look, Jesus—you seem to be a great teacher, but now you're talking about my area of expertise. Fishing is my business. What you're asking us to do isn't practical. Besides, it's going to be a lot of hard work, and we'll probably have to pay overtime." Michael laughed.

"I think that's a pretty good interpretation," said the Minister. "Let's read on:

> "When they had done so, they caught such a large number of fish that their nets began to break. So they signaled their partners in the other boat to come and help them, and they came and filled both boats so full that they began to sink."

"I get the hint," Michael said. "So you're suggesting Jesus knows my business, too."

"Yes," the Minister said. "Jesus knows your business, and he can help. And if you're going to turn an operation as complicated as the Baxter Center around, you could use his help. That means you have to trust his wisdom."

Michael paused, then asked, "Would you be willing to coach me?"

Now it was the Minister's turn to pause. "Well," he answered, "the professional methods that I've told you about, even though Jesus practiced them, are out of my expertise. Why don't I call my professor friend and see if he'll join us. Maybe between the two of us, with Jesus as our model and guide, we can be of some help."

"Fabulous," said Michael.

* * *

"I'll never forget how excited we were the first time the three of us met," the Professor said.

The Minister agreed. "Here was our opportunity to see how the concepts of character and method, with Jesus as the model, could impact a leader's success and effectiveness in a turnaround project."

"By that time," the Professor recalled, "Michael had learned even more of what he'd gotten himself into with the Baxter Center, and he admitted to feeling more than a little nervous."

"Yes," said the Minister, smiling, "but then I remember Michael telling us, 'With the two of you in my corner, I'm ready to go.' That's when I reminded him not to forget his third partner. He smiled and said, 'That's right—our boats are headed for deep water!' "

The Professor and the Minister recalled the frequent meetings the three of them had during the several weeks prior to Michael's taking over the Baxter Center. Michael played the student's role while the two others shared the role of coach and consultant. The Minister concentrated on teaching about the importance of character and the meaning of servant leadership and discipleship. The Professor focused on leadership methods.

"But you know," said the Professor, "it didn't take long before we all were learners."

"Those meetings certainly began to influence me," said the Minister. "I started making changes in my leadership style within the church. By looking at Jesus through your eyes, and being aware for the first time of his leadership methods as well as his message, I found new hope for meeting the needs of my congregation without me in the center of everything."

"I, too, experienced a change in my thinking and teaching as a result of our work with Michael," said the Professor. "I began by making references to the character side of servant leadership in my writing and speeches—tentative references at first, but then with increasing confidence and excitement. As I spoke about the compatibility of my leadership theories with the servant leadership practiced by Jesus, I was amazed at the response. Some of my friends and readers counseled against tampering with the formula that had been so successful in the past. Others, however, responded like people dying of thirst who had just been given a cool drink of water."

"So we were all learning," said the Minister. "It was truly a case of one plus one plus one equaling greater than three."

9

Spiritual Significance Versus Earthly Success

A nurse interrupted their reminiscing to say that Carla was on the phone. The Professor stepped down the hall to the nurse's desk to take the call.

"I know you'd call me here at home if you had any news," Carla said. "But before going to bed I just had to check: Have you heard anything from the doctors or nurses?"

"No," said the Professor, "it's been very quiet here. We're still praying that Michael recovers—and when he does, Carla, we'll never let him drift away so far again. We're taking your request seriously. We've been having a long talk about the things we've taught him before and what really matters. This time we'll help him stay on track."

Carla expressed her gratitude, then added, "Allison and I have been talking as well. Your wife is quite a woman—the best counselor I've ever had. She helps me see the bigger picture and the possibility of something good coming out of all of this."

"The big picture is what we all need now," said the Professor. "That's how we'll get through this." Before hanging up, the Professor reassured Carla that they would call her the minute there was any news about Michael's condition.

When the Professor rejoined the Minister, they talked about Michael's quick intellectual grasp of everything they taught him.

"I remember coming to the conclusion," said the Professor, "that if anyone had a clear understanding in their head about what servant leadership is all about, it had to be Michael."

"And yet it wasn't always easy for Michael. He had trouble in his heart and with his hands," said the Minister. "At first his hard-driving temperament and impatience for results made his attempts at serving the needs of his people a hit-and-miss affair."

"I remember that after you shared with him the servant leadership modeled by Jesus," said the Professor, "he was hungry to know more about what a person with a servant heart was like. He knew it was contrary to what was in his heart."

"Yes," said the Minister. "That was an important conversation for the three of us. I recall telling him . . ."

* * *

"People with servant hearts have certain characteristics and values in common as they make leadership decisions. *Their paramount aim is the best interests of those they lead.*"

"In other words," said Michael, "personal power, recognition, or money is never the focus."

"Never," insisted the Minister. "That's why servant leaders are willing to share power. Their purpose is to equip other people to become freer, more autonomous, more capable—and therefore more effective."

"Servant leaders must get *personal satisfaction from watching the growth and development of those they lead,*" observed the Professor.

"Exactly," continued the Minister. "When you combine that attribute with having *a loving care for those they lead,* you know you're dealing with a different kind of leader."

"That's interesting. But how about accountability?" asked Michael.

"Leaders with servant hearts *want to be held accountable for their behavior and results,*" said the Minister. "They want to know whether they have been helpful to those they're serving."

"I bet that means they *are willing to listen,*" commented the Professor.

"That's a given," said the Minister. "They receive criticism and advice as a gift even when it isn't offered for positive reasons. Anything you say that will help them do a better job is welcome. After all, their aim is to serve."

"This all sounds great," said Michael, "but what keeps servant leaders from going crazy trying to please everyone?"

"I know some people think that's what servant leadership is all about—pleasing everyone," said the Professor. "That couldn't be farther from the truth. And it's one of the great principles that Jesus demonstrated."

"Jesus certainly didn't try to please everyone," said the Minister. "His single concern in his leadership was to please God. To me, true servant leaders want to serve and help people to accomplish their goals and be effective, but ultimately they're seeking to please only one—the Lord."

"That certainly presents a different focus for a leader," said Michael. "But don't you think all this talk about God could turn some people off?"

"It might," said the Minister. "But I'm convinced that not admitting there's a God makes about as much sense as saying the unabridged dictionary was the result of an explosion in a print shop."

"That's a good one." Michael laughed.

"More to your point," said the Minister, "being a servant leader without a relationship with God can become just another ego trip."

"Could you explain that further?" wondered Michael.

The Minister pulled out a pen and turned to a blank page in his Pocket Planner. On the blank page he wrote the words "E.G.O. = *E*dging *G*od *O*ut" and handed it to Michael.

"So, to be a servant leader, you can't have a big ego," commented Michael.

"Precisely," said the Minister. "As a leader, we're called to serve. If we accept that calling, good results will follow. People tend to exceed expectations when they're led by someone who cares about them and has their best interests in mind. Without a relationship with the caller—God has been edged out—people tend to get prideful and start to think they deserve the credit when the results and the applause come. True servant leaders know where the credit belongs."

"I heard recently that 'E.G.O.' could also represent another phrase," said the Professor. "*E*verything *G*ood *O*utside. When people's egos take control, they become other-directed and determine and evaluate who they are by external rewards, not internal peace."

"That's for sure," said the Minister. "And an emphasis on obedience to a higher mission and set of values, which Jesus lived, requires keeping one's ego under control. A big ego can't coexist with a servant heart because it puts concern for self ahead of service to others and pleasing God. You start thinking that the sheep are there for the benefit of the shepherd. And that mind-set soon begins to negatively impact the rest of your life. The Scripture says: 'God opposes the proud but gives grace to the humble.' "

"Leaders with servant hearts by definition have *genuine humility,*" continued the Minister, "but they also have confidence. They don't think less of themselves, they just think about themselves less. Their egos don't *Edge God Out.* In fact, their primary concern is for spiritual significance rather than earthly success."

"What's the difference between spiritual significance and earthly success?" inquired Michael.

"Leaders who focus on earthly success," replied the Minister, "are usually driven by three main desires that have undermined leaders since the beginning of time: power, recognition, and greed."

"I think that maintaining power is particularly important to most leaders, isn't it?" asked the Professor.

"I agree," said the Minister. "Power and status seem to be their main motivators. That's why many leaders want to hold on to their leadership positions at any and all costs."

"Wasn't Jesus tempted with power and status?" asked Michael.

"Yes," said the Minister. "The Bible tells how the devil took Jesus to a mountaintop and showed him all the kingdoms of the world and their glory. 'All this I will give you,' the devil said, 'if you will bow down and worship me.' But Jesus overcame this temptation by reaffirming that his first loyalty was to God."

"That certainly highlights that servant leadership is not about pleasing everyone, but only pleasing one," said Michael. "I would assume the same could be said of recognition and greed."

"Most certainly," said the Minister. "Jesus confronted the danger of seeking recognition in his Sermon on the Mount, where he said, 'Be careful not to do your "acts of righteousness" before men, to be seen by them. If you do, you will have no reward from your Father in Heaven.'

"All throughout the Bible we see warnings about the allurement of money; the most memorable passage for me is 'For the love of money is a root of all kinds of evil.' "

"Wait a minute," said Michael. "Are you saying that money is bad?"

"Not in and of itself," said the Minister. "Just like profit isn't bad in and of itself. It's the love of money at the exclusion of all else that's the problem. That's when you forget about what's really important—your relationships—starting with your relationship with God and moving eventually to the key people in your life. Making money is good and necessary for your family, but make sure your family doesn't get lost in the shuffle. Making profit is good and necessary for the financial strength of your company, but make sure you don't forget about serving your customers and creating a motivating environment for the people you manage."

"Another problem with the earthly success factors that so many leaders pursue," interjected the Professor, "is that they set you up for frustration and disappointment. Someone else always has more power, more recognition, more money."

"So focusing on the earthly success game is an endless battle," Michael said. "You're trying to keep up with the Joneses. I heard one person complain, 'How can I keep up with my neighbors when they keep on buying things I can't afford?' "

"That's where spiritual significance is different," said the Minister, laughing. "It's not about competition or winning. It's about who you are in your relationship to God. Jesus taught his followers that there was a world of difference between being rich on the inside and being rich in monetary terms. Inner riches—a vital relationship with God—produce the kind of peace that people long for. But the drive for external power, recognition, or wealth so often creates more problems than it solves."

Michael nodded. "I can see that spiritual significance brings a truly different focus to leadership."

"I've been fascinated to realize," continued the Minister, "that leaders driven by one or more of the earthly desires can never realize spiritual significance. They're focused on the wrong things. They try to overcome their spiritual emptiness by striving to hold on to control and maintaining their leadership position at any cost."

"But I would predict," intervened the Professor, "that leaders who focus on spiritual significance factors can still achieve earthly success."

"On that point," said the Minister, "Jesus provided us with a clear message about having a primary focus on issues of spiritual significance. When he cautioned against being overly anxious about earthly matters in the Sermon on the Mount, Jesus told the crowds: 'But seek first his Kingdom and his righteousness and all these things will be given to you as well.' "

"In other words," replied Michael, "when you focus on the right thing, right results are probable."

"C. S. Lewis said it well," interjected the Minister. " 'Aim at Heaven and you will get "earth thrown in." Aim at earth and you will get neither.' "

"That reminds me of an interesting experiment I saw recently," said the Professor. "I was speaking at a seminar with a sports psychologist. He asked the participants if there was anyone in the audience who couldn't catch a ball. A woman raised her hand.

"The sports psychologist took a big soft Nerf ball and said to the woman, 'I'm going to throw this ball toward you. See if you can catch it.'

"Every time he threw it, she bobbled it and the ball fell to the floor. She obviously couldn't catch.

"Then the sports psychologist told her, 'This time when I throw the ball toward you, don't worry about catching it. Instead, focus on the number of times the ball fully rotates from the time it leaves my hand until it gets to you.'

"This time when he threw the ball, she caught it every time while calling out 'four' or 'three'—the number of times the ball rotated before it got to her. When she realized what she was doing, the woman asked in amazement, 'Why can I catch the ball now?'

"He answered her, 'Because you weren't focused on the results—whether you caught the ball or not. You were focusing only on the process—how many times the ball rotated. This relaxed you and you stopped worrying, which permitted you to get good results. You started catching the ball.' "

"So focusing all your attention on results can also get you in trouble?" wondered Michael.

"Yes," said the Professor. "Both personally and professionally."

"That really hits home," said Michael. "I think that's what I was doing in my work. All my energy has been directed toward the bottom line—the profit margin. While that has usually produced good results in the short run, and pleased the owners, I've heard rumblings from my customers and people. In retrospect, I realize that always catches up with you in the long run."

"I once heard profit defined as *the applause you get from creating raving-fan customers through gung-ho people,*" said the Professor. "Raving-fan customers are people who are so excited about how they get treated by your people that they want to brag about you. They become like part of your sales force. Gung-ho people act like they're owners. They're willing to go the extra mile for customers. They know the company leaders trust and respect their contributions."

"I like that," said Michael. "And if you have raving-fan customers and gung-ho people, I imagine your cash registers will go *ka-ching, ka-ching, ka-ching.*"

"That's for sure," said the Professor.

"So if I understand what you're saying," said Michael, "God is far more concerned with our character and our leadership process than he is with our earthly success factors."

"Yes," the Minister answered. "Mother Teresa used to say, 'We are called to obedience, not to success.' "

"She certainly was focused on spiritual significance, wasn't she?" said Michael.

"She was simply following Jesus' example in her particular vocation," said the Minister. "Being generous, having a servant heart, serving others, developing loving relationships—that's how Jesus calls all of us to live our life. Not only will you get a 'Well done, good and faithful servant' when life's over, but also perhaps good earthly results as well.

"But let us be very clear, there's no guarantee of getting the kind of positive earthly results we typically think about. God may have something different in mind for you. In fact, a friend of mine recently observed, 'If you want to hear God laugh, tell him *your plan.*' "

10

The Heart of the Matter

It was at one of their next meetings that Michael asked several questions that were to have life-changing significance for him, the Minister, and the Professor and their understanding of the dynamics of the head, heart, and hands of Jesus-like leadership.

After updating the Minister and Professor regarding his first few weeks at the Baxter Center, Michael leaned forward in the restaurant booth where they were having lunch. "There are a few things I have been wondering about throughout our discussions that I need some help with," said Michael. "First of all, we have talked a lot about having a servant heart as a key requirement to lead as Jesus would lead.

"If you look at all the leaders in positions of influence today, you would have to conclude," continued Michael, "that a servant heart doesn't come as original equipment. With all the material goodies of power, recognition, and wealth potentially available without one, why would anyone want a servant heart? And more importantly, if you wanted one, how could you get it?"

After bowing his head for a moment as the open honesty of Michael's question filled his mind and heart, the Minister responded. "Michael," he said, "your questions go right to the core issues involved in Jesus-like leadership. You're absolutely right when you say that a servant heart isn't part of our original equipment. To continue the analogy, I believe our 'original equipment' heart is one that operates in a way that promotes and protects our own self-interest as its primary focus. It pumps a continual stream of pride, ego, and fear into our thoughts and actions. It calculates the answer to 'What's in it for me?' at the speed of light and triggers our rapid response system to the world around us just as fast."

"It doesn't sound too pretty," said Michael, "or very hopeful."

"Not if left in place," replied the Minister. "But there is very good news regarding replacement equipment," he said with a smile.

"Please continue," said the Professor.

"Very well," said the Minister. "I believe we were created by an unconditionally loving God. But when we enter life, we develop a kind of amnesia. We forget where we came from—our heritage. It takes us various amounts of time to return to home base—recognition of our heritage and God's unconditional love.

"I believe that until we return home, we have a fundamental yearning—an emptiness—that cannot be filled as long as we operate within the limitations of an unchanged heart. That yearning is for unconditional love and acceptance. No earthly success or recognition can fill it—only a relationship with God, made possible through what Christ did on the cross. A true servant heart is the by-product of a life surrendered in gratitude to the transforming power of God's unconditional love and forgiveness. The desire to honor the giver of that love through service to him as Jesus modeled is the primary ambition and animating force of a transformed servant heart."

"So what you're saying is that you can't just decide to have a change of heart. It has to happen to you," said Michael.

"Yes," said the Minister. "It has to happen through the transforming work of Jesus. As much as people are into self-improvement these days, this is the one operation that can only be performed by God when all the trying is done and there is unconditional surrender."

"It sounds simple, but difficult," replied Michael.

"Right on both points," said the Minister. "There is a freewill decision to make. Jesus will never impose himself on anyone. But bending the knee and saying, 'Your way, not mine' are two of the hardest acts for people to accomplish, especially ego-driven leaders with 'original equipment' hearts. But these are the keys to a transformed life."

"Suppose as the leader of an organization," wondered Michael, "I surrender. I get back to home base and recognize God's unconditional love. Before I implement servant leadership throughout my organization, do I have to convert everyone?"

"Absolutely not," insisted the Minister. "The best advice I've heard on that subject is: 'In sharing your faith, use words only when necessary.' In other words, the best way you can share your faith is to behave differently as a leader."

"Good point," said the Professor. "If you started requiring or suggesting that your managers should be servant leaders and live their lives as Jesus would lead them to do, they're likely to revolt, particularly if they don't believe in a Supreme Being, or if the God they believe in is not *your* God. Instead, I suggest you establish a clear vision and set of operating values consistent with the principles of servant leadership. No one will disagree with the values inherent in servant leadership. In fact, they'll embrace them.

"Once these values are agreed upon (and values need to be agreed upon—they can't be mandated) and behaviorally defined, employees within the organization must be expected to behave in a manner consistent with these definitions. Now the values become the boss."

"That's interesting," said Michael. "But many organizations either don't have a set of operating values, or if they do, they're followed by leaders only when it's convenient. When egos get in the way, values seem to go out the window."

"Without a set of operating values," continued the Professor, "that are clearly defined and enforced—people are expected to behave according to them—you're at the mercy of people's good intentions. Great leaders don't create optional cultures. For example, it isn't optional to be friendly to customers and serve them well or to treat people within the organization with respect.

"I think you would be amazed," said the Professor, "that once behavioral norms are established and fulfilled, how quickly people's hearts will be softened and their individual innate characteristics will take the form of caring for and serving others."

"And once this step is taken," interjected the Minister, "the door is open for people to explore a closer connection with God."

"So you both think that when the student is ready the teacher will appear," said Michael. "And the process of servant leadership could actually have a dramatic impact on those who do not believe in God or follow in the footsteps of Jesus."

The Professor and Minister both nodded in agreement.

* * *

Despite the late hour, the Professor and the Minister continued to recall the many seeds of servant leadership that were already planted in Michael's mind and had started to soften his heart. They continued to explore together how to bring them back to life.

Finally the Professor looked through a small window high in the wall above the waiting room, and noticed that the sky's color had changed from black to an early-dawn gray.

"I haven't had a good all-night discussion like this since I was an undergraduate," he said.

"Same here," the Minister answered as he followed the Professor's gaze to the morning's first light.

11

The Awakening

Just as the Minister and the Professor were catching a glimpse of dawn from the hospital's upper-story windows, Carla and Allison were watching the same morning sky through the bay window beside Carla's breakfast table.

Carla had just concluded a brief phone conversation with one of Michael's doctors at the hospital. He was planning to confer shortly with his associates, then wanted to meet with Carla a little later in the morning to discuss their diagnosis.

She was anxious to return to Michael's side, but Allison had prepared coffee and a light breakfast and had encouraged Carla to sit down for a few quiet moments before rushing off for another stressful day at the hospital. Allison sat in silence beside her, not trying to force any conversation, but ready to listen and offer comfort where she could.

Both women gazed out the window at the graceful forms of tree branches revealed in the growing light. After a while, Carla quietly spoke up.

"You know, I keep rehashing what the doctor said and how he said it. He didn't really sound discouraged. But I just wish he'd told me more, even if it was bad news."

"Well," Allison responded calmly, "he did say Michael's condition had stabilized. That's got to be about the best news possible at this point. And there's bound to be more after the doctors have talked everything over. I'm sure they just want to be very certain about whatever they tell you."

Carla nodded, the lines of worry lessening a bit on her forehead. She took another sip of coffee, then lowered the cup. With both hands she gripped its warmth more tightly. She glanced down at her slender fingers wrapped through the cup handle, and stared at her wedding band.

"But then again," she said slowly, "the doctor made it clear that Michael isn't out of danger yet."

Her tears came again. "Oh, Allison, I know in my heart Michael is going to be okay, but it's hard. I'm just not sure I'm strong enough for this!"

"That's why God has us here," Allison reassured her. "To help you be strong, Carla, as we know you really are. And remember that we're praying, and we'll keep it up."

Carla managed a grateful smile for her friend as the first rays of the sunrise sparkled in the window.

A few hours later, Allison, the Professor, and the Minister were at Carla's side as the doctor gave his report. The news was promising: Michael's condition had stabilized enough that the doctors were considering bypass surgery the following morning. They had a fair degree of confidence that the procedure could restore him to health. Meanwhile, they would continue assessing and monitoring his condition. "For the moment," the doctor told them, "it's important to keep him as quiet and undisturbed as possible. Carla, you can stay with him, but I'd prefer that the rest of you"—looking at Allison, the Professor, and the Minister—"remain in the waiting room."

* * *

Late that afternoon, Michael woke up, though he had no sense of the time. For the first time he began to connect more meaning to the signs and sounds around him. The heart monitor continued its monotonous but reassuring *ping.* The pain in his chest, so excruciating at the fitness center, had retreated into a dull, deep ache. From somewhere—out in the hallway, he guessed—he heard muffled voices.

Then he noticed Carla asleep in a chair pulled close to his bed. Her hand lay loosely near his, and she was nodding forward as if she had just fallen asleep in the middle of something important.

A wave of sadness and affection for Carla filled Michael's eyes with hot tears. How could he have let this beautiful woman slip from the center of his life into the role of a supporting cast member in his ego trip? He wanted to tell her again how sorry he was for isolating himself in his business life and for putting their relationship on prolonged hold. He wanted to hold her close and win back the warmth and closeness they had shared before his career took precedence over everything else.

He started to speak. But sensing Carla's exhaustion, he decided not to disturb her just yet.

As he settled his head back on the pillow, he willed himself to think.

During all the success he'd known in recent years, Michael had assumed his family was getting along pretty well, despite the compression of their life together into a series of quick sound-bite time slots on weekends.

Not long ago they had taken their annual vacation to Carla's father's fishing camp in Wyoming—where, at least for two weeks, life moved at a less intense pace. But this year Michael had to take lots of work with him, and the invasion of their vacation time brought out obvious tensions in their family. Michael could no longer escape the signs of it.

He forced open his eyes, turning again to look at Carla.

This time his eyes caught hers.

"Michael!"

At once she was at his side. He felt her warm palms on his cheeks, and gazed into her moist eyes.

He tried turning his shoulders so he could reach out to her, but a shot of pain through his chest pulled him back.

Before dropping into sleep again, he heard her voice once more: "You'll be okay, Michael. I'm with you, and together with God we'll get through this."

12

The Recovery

Michael's surgery the next morning took just under three hours. When it was over, the Minister, the Professor, and Allison were at Carla's side to hear the surgeon report that the operation appeared to have gone well.

It was not until the next day that his doctor decided to allow his friends in to see Michael, and it would be for only a brief visit, allowing Michael to continue reserving his strength for his body's healing. While the Professor and the Minister were at the hospital, Allison went with Carla to pick up her kids.

When Michael saw his two old friends, a genuine smile lit up his pale and gaunt face. As he shook hands with the Professor and the Minister, he joked, "I remember you guys used to talk about *heart attack,* but maybe this isn't what you had in mind."

"Not really," said the Minister, smiling, "but we're glad to see you back on the road to recovery."

"Now that you're out of danger," said the Professor, "we've decided to return home. But we'll certainly keep in touch."

"I want to thank you for being here," said Michael. "I know you had to set aside a lot of deserving commitments and obligations to be here for me and for Carla. I just can't thank you both and Allison enough for that!"

"Better that," the Professor said, smiling, "than having to carve out time for your funeral."

"It's been a close call, for sure," Michael acknowledged. "And because of it, I feel I have so much to talk to you about, and I don't know where to start—except with one word: Help. I think I may need it now more than I ever did back when we were together."

"We happen to have plenty of ideas about that," the Minister said. "Thanks to Carla's encouragement, we've been making the most of the hours we spent in that waiting room down the hall. Planning how to help you for the long haul was the only item on our agenda."

"As soon as you're up for it," said the Professor, "we'll schedule our own personal retreat—just the three of us—to explore the options together."

Michael's expression conveyed his intense relief at hearing his friends' commitment. "It sounds like we're going to be a team again," he told them. "And I like that!"

13

The Retreat

Six weeks later, just before Michael was to return to work, the three friends agreed to meet at the lakeside cottage that the Minister and Peggy used as their refuge from the constantly pressing responsibilities of their ministry.

House rules set decades before kept the cottage free of TV. The only means of communication with the outside world were a single unimproved phone line and the daily mail boat. The slow-paced flow of activities, plus local friendships renewed each year, made for a cherished antidote to the busy world that lay just down the road and out of sight.

While the Minister played an occasional golf game here, his real passion when he was near the water was sailing. He exercised this passion with a colorful crew of local saints and sinners.

Peggy, though, enjoyed the prolonged periods of quiet she was able to snatch between the comings and goings of her family. She loved to walk the dogs, and to create new plots and adventures for the series of children's stories she wrote for a national magazine.

The Minister, the Professor, and Michael had met at the cottage several times during the days of the Baxter Center project and found it very conducive to dialogue and solitude. It would be the perfect setting for renewing their involvement together.

On the date when the Professor and Michael were to join him there, the Minister had busied himself throughout the day making final preparations for closing up the cottage for the end of the summer season. That was his chore, while Peggy had headed home earlier that morning with the kids to get them ready for the fall opening of school. Since she and the kids had been away all summer, either at the cottage or in Dallas, much had to be done.

Michael and the Professor were due to arrive around dinnertime. It was still warm enough to eat outside, so the Minister decided to treat his friends to one of his rustic barbecues, which had been so popular during their previous visits to the lake.

As the sun dropped behind the nearby trees, the Minister started the charcoal in the ancient outdoor grill. He watched the pieces of charcoal begin to catch fire at the edge of the pile in the grill. The sight reminded him of an illustration he'd used with his congregation to explain the need for community in the spiritual life of an individual. He asked them to imagine a fire much like this one, with every piece of charcoal burning brightly. Then he asked them to imagine a piece falling away from the pile. Once out of touch with the others, the solitary piece of charcoal would burn brightly on its own for a little while, then slowly cool, and eventually die out completely—only half-used.

It was like that with Michael, the Minister thought. Once Michael drifted away from their fellowship with the Professor, he hadn't been able to sustain his spiritual walk as a leader. The lure of recognition, power, and greed is always present, particularly when you're a leader like Michael and have some real successes to *E*dge *G*od *O*ut and get you off course.

The Minister and the Professor had talked on the phone a number of times after they left New York and Michael's bedside. They agreed that one critically important thing they had learned from Michael's situation was that the right kind of leadership—the leadership that best serves others and God—is a one-day-at-a-time process. It's a daily walking in faith. In fact, the Professor called it *FaithWalk* Leadership.

That's what the Minister and Professor had hoped Michael would continue to do—walk his faith day by day in the marketplace. They agreed that *FaithWalk* Leadership involves first getting healthy in our leadership role with Jesus as a model, then staying that way despite the constant and varied temptations to think and act in an unhealthy manner, with our ego taking the lead.

The Minister realized that the Professor and he were naïve enough to think that once Michael recognized the relationship between his faith and how he should act as a leader, he would never lose sight of it. But he did, and so do most well-intentioned leaders. That's why the Professor and the Minister were exploring the idea of establishing a Center for *FaithWalk* Leadership to help leaders like Michael stay the course.

"That's where we let Michael down," reflected the Minister. "When he moved away, we weren't able to provide consistent support and encouragement to help him combat the temptations confronting him on a daily basis. He needed friendly, caring pressure to stay on course. We simply assumed that he would remember the good news—the VERY GOOD NEWS—that he was not alone and didn't have to be. Not only did he have us, but more importantly, he had Him."

The image that came to the Minister's mind when he thought about the Center for *FaithWalk* Leadership and what Michael needed was a tugboat and how it moves a big ocean liner around the harbor. A tugboat doesn't go 2,000 yards away, rev up its engines, then come in with full-force power and slam into the liner to get it to move. That would be disastrous. Instead, a tugboat comes alongside and applies constant pressure over an extended period of time. That's the only way it's going to move the liner.

That's what Michael needed—friendly, caring pressure. And yet, when they felt resistance from Michael, the Minister and Professor had given up on him and weren't there for him.

The Professor told the Minister, "And we knew better. At least, I should have. I have learned over the years that even when you have thoroughly trained people, you don't completely turn your back on them. That would be abdicating. With effective delegating, you stay in touch with people enough to know if they need you."

"I should have known better, too," thought the Minister. "After Jesus delegates 'the great commission' to his disciples, as recorded at the end of Matthew's gospel, he tells them: 'And surely, I am with you always, to the very end of the age.'

"Jesus is always there for us when we need him. We weren't there for Michael," he realized, "and without our reinforcement his communication with Jesus became ceremonial again, and not on a day-to-day basis."

The Minister vowed not to let this happen a second time, even if it meant setting up weekly conference calls between the three men. A verse from the ancient wisdom of the Book of Ecclesiastes sprang to mind:

> Two are better than one, because they have a good return for their work: If one falls down, his friend can help him up. But pity the man who falls and has no one to help him up! Also, if two lie down together, they will keep warm. But how can one keep warm alone? Though one may be overpowered, two can defend themselves. A cord of three strands is not quickly broken.

The sound of a car stopping on the gravel driveway announced that Michael and the Professor had arrived. They had flown in from different directions and met at the airport.

"Welcome," said the Minister as Michael got out of the car looking fit and well-rested despite the all-day journey. "I hope you're ready for a pretty thorough going-over before we let you loose on the world again."

"Well, considering that you almost had the chance to conduct my funeral service, I guess I'll be able to stand the heat," replied Michael with a smile.

"I hope the treatment isn't going to include any trials by sailboat," chimed in the Professor as he began to retrieve the bags from the trunk.

"You're lucky this time," said the Minister. "We took the boat out for the season yesterday. But I could still arrange a four- or five-hour sail in one of the neighbors' boats if you're interested."

"No, thanks. We wouldn't want you to go to all that trouble," replied the Professor with a chuckle. "Michael and I were just reminiscing about the first time you talked us into being part of the crew for one of your little afternoon races."

"That was a real ego-buster," said Michael. "I never remember feeling so useless and helpless. Floundering like a bug on its back while you were calmly putting us into harm's way."

"It was the first time that my bum knee became an asset for survival," said the Professor, laughing, who had landed a cushy sitdown job on the now infamous trip.

"Well, if you change your minds, just let me know," said the Minister. "Come on in and stow your gear and help me put the finishing touches on this dinner."

14
A Choice

After a leisurely meal during which the three friends caught up on all the comings and goings of their families, they sat in the gathering darkness on the porch staring out at the moon's glow on the lake. The Minister was the first to break the silence.

"Michael, how are you feeling about facing the lions in the streets again?" he inquired.

"From a physical standpoint, I feel like a lean mean fighting machine, thanks to Carla's tough loving care that kept me honest on all my rehab activities," Michael replied. "But to be honest, I'm a little apprehensive about facing the level of pressure I know is waiting for me."

"That's something we wanted to talk to you about," said the Minister. "The Professor and I have an alternative suggestion to your going back into the fire that we thought you might want to consider."

"What is it?" wondered Michael.

"We're thinking about creating a Center for *FaithWalk* Leadership to help leaders of faith like yourself to recalibrate their commitment to spiritual significance on a daily basis so they don't relapse into serving themselves rather than serving God or people."

"Tell me more," said Michael.

"As we've learned with you," said the Minister, "when you try to help someone change his head, his heart, and his hands or behavior, you have to stay in touch. You can't abdicate. That person periodically needs support and even occasional coaching."

"That's for sure," Michael agreed.

"We were even fantasizing," said the Professor, smiling, "that we would start an AA-like twelve-step program designed to deal with the ego issues of *FaithWalk* leaders."

"I can see it now," the Minister said, laughing. "A room full of people standing up one at a time and saying, 'Hi, I'm John, and I am an ego-driven leader. It's been three weeks since my ego needs and drive for earthly success got too much, and I . . .' "

"That could certainly scare some people off," said the Professor. "But when you think about it, the disciplines included in the typical twelve-step program are in keeping with the end goal of *FaithWalk* Leadership: helping leaders like Michael continue to act on their good intentions as servant leaders and to develop their own strategy to combat the temptations to do otherwise that will undoubtedly continue to bombard them at work and at home."

"Have you thought about what those twelve steps might involve?" Michael wondered.

"Yes, we have them written down," said the Minister as he handed a sheet of paper to Michael.

Twelve Steps to *FaithWalk* Leadership

1. I admit that on more than one occasion I have allowed my ego needs and drive for earthly success to impact my role as a leader—and that my leadership has not been the servant leadership that Jesus modeled.
2. I've come to believe that God can transform my leadership motives, thoughts, and actions to the servant leadership that Jesus modeled.
3. I've made a decision to turn my leadership efforts over to God, and to become an apprentice of Jesus and the servant leadership he modeled.
4. I've made a searching and fearless inventory of my leadership motives, thoughts, and behaviors that are inconsistent with servant leadership.
5. I've admitted to God, to myself, and to at least one other person the exact nature of my leadership gaps—when I behave in ways that do not make Jesus proud.
6. I am entirely ready to have God remove all character defects that have created gaps in my leadership.

7. I humbly ask God to remove my shortcomings and to strengthen me against the temptations of recognition, power, and greed.
8. I've made a list of people whom I may have harmed by my ego-driven leadership, and I am willing to make amends to them all.
9. I've made direct amends to such people whenever possible, unless doing so would injure them or others.
10. I continue to take personal inventory regarding my leadership role, and when I am wrong, I promptly admit it.
11. By engaging the disciplines of solitude, prayer, and study of the Scriptures, I seek to align my servant leadership efforts with what Jesus modeled, and to constantly seek ways to be a servant first and a leader second with the people I encounter in my leadership responsibilities.
12. Having had a "heart attack" regarding the principles of servant leadership, I have tried to carry this message to other leaders, and to practice them in all my affairs.

"That would be quite a program for a leader to attempt," Michael said. "Would the Center for *FaithWalk* Leadership be open to leaders who were not followers of Jesus?"

"Sure," said the Professor, "as long as they understood that the model for *FaithWalk* Leadership is Jesus, and the textbook is the Bible. *FaithWalk* Leadership isn't about converting leaders to Christianity, but about helping them to become the kind of leader Jesus was and to align their leader behavior with the servant leadership values that he modeled."

"I like your thinking," said Michael. "The process you're suggesting will impact the head, the heart, and the hands of leaders."

"And it's a way to combine the strengths of each of our domains," said the Minister, "my focus on character development, and the Professor's focus on leadership methods. In fact, by bringing together the character dimensions inherent in servant leadership as modeled by Jesus with the leadership methods the Professor has been teaching, I see two practical benefits: First of all, it provides an effective way for followers of Jesus, as well as some of his admirers, to infuse his thinking into their daily actions and relationships in the workplace.

"And the second benefit," continued the Minister, "is that since the leadership concepts taught by the Professor describe how Jesus wanted his followers to carry out their leadership responsibility, they provide an effective leadership model for the work of the church."

"That's the win-win aspect of the Center for *FaithWalk* Leadership," said the Professor. "What we wanted to know, Michael, is if you would be interested in working with us on this project? We need someone to make our services available to business leaders such as yourself, as well as church leaders, and begin to create a network of support and accountability groups throughout the country. The purpose of these groups is to help people in leadership roles to live out all aspects of Jesus-like leadership."

"That sounds fascinating," Michael said. "While I want to support your efforts, I think I should get back on the horse and see if I can become an effective leader in my present job and not let my ego get me off course there or at home. I owe it to the people at work and to Carla, the kids, and to myself . . . and I guess to you guys as well."

"We half-expected that would be your answer, and we'll leave the door open for you to join us at a later date," said the Minister.

"And you're absolutely right that we have a major stake in all this," chimed in the Professor. "It would be pretty embarrassing for your high-powered mentors if you blow it again. As they say, 'Blow it once, shame on you. Blow it twice, shame on us.' "

"Okay," said Michael sheepishly. "I'll try and protect your reputations a little better this time."

15
Checking the Heart

"Excellent," said the Minister, "and to be sure you do, we're going to fully equip you for the job before you leave here. So let's get at it."

"What do you have in mind?" asked Michael.

"Well," said the Minister, "I think we should treat you the same way we do when we're about to launch a boat that's been in dry dock for a major overhaul and refitting. We want to see if you're seaworthy."

"I don't know," said the Professor. "This sounds a little suspicious."

"Trust me. I think it will help," said the Minister.

"Okay, Captain, I'm game," said Michael. "Where do we start?"

"Well," said the Minister, "first we're going to make sure you're rid of all the mental barnacles that could be affecting your ability to live your life as a servant leader."

"Just for the record, Michael, what went wrong after you moved to New York?" asked the Professor.

"That's a question I pondered when I first woke up in the hospital, and have been thinking about ever since," said Michael. "When I boil it all down, it was a combination of ego and self-imposed isolation."

"Please explain," said the Minister.

"Sure," said Michael. "During our time together, when I was involved in the Baxter Center Project, I was not so sure I knew all the answers and was on my knees almost daily praying for guidance and hoping the new methods I was applying would work.

"When I went to New York with the Baxter Center Project as my major calling card," Michael continued, "I started trying to catch lightning in a bottle a second time. I was asked to breathe life into another complacent family conglomerate that needed radical transformation to make it competitive again. But this company differed from Baxter in three ways: It was larger, it was more complicated, and it was publicly traded.

"It quickly became obvious that the company needed radical surgery to boost growth and revive its stock, which had long underperformed in the bullish market. Less profitable business units had to be spun off and new ventures bought to support the performing ones. As the pressure built, I began to panic and manage for the short run. I let fear of failure and my pride rule my thinking. I lost track of the fact that I was secure and safe in God's unconditional love. I became completely focused on pleasing only one constituency: the shareholders.

"In the process, without realizing it," said Michael, "I started to manage my reputation instead of guarding my soul. The more praise I received from the stockholders and the Wall Street crowd, the harder I worked and the more credit I let myself take as being something special. It was a high ride, and I liked it."

"What do you mean when you say you started to manage your reputation?" asked the Professor.

"As I think back, it had a seemingly insignificant beginning," replied Michael. "It started with some slight annoyance when I received negative feedback on something I'd put into motion, or when people didn't get the big picture the first time I explained it to them.

"As I drove myself and those around me to live up to the expectations of 'Michael the Great,' I became increasingly impatient and eventually downright intolerant of anything or anybody that wasted my time. If it didn't serve my purposes—purposes that in my mind were always wonderful and pure—I made anyone's negative feedback painful for them, or else regarded it as an act of disrespect. As you warned might happen, I began to act as if the sheep were there for the benefit of the shepherd."

"Unfortunately, that happens to a lot of managers," said the Professor.

"I knew that," Michael said, "but, nevertheless, the temptation of that kind of thinking began to take over my mind. It wasn't something I became consciously aware of at the time, but it took a major toll on me and on those around me, including Carla and the kids."

"How so?" the Minister asked.

"As the external applause became more and more important to sustain, I began to put everything else in my life on extended hold, including my closest relationships. That's why I stopped answering your calls."

"So that's why," the Professor said, laughing. "We just thought you didn't like us anymore."

"Not really." Michael smiled. "I think it was more about not liking myself. In time, as each project took over my attention, I became more and more intolerant of people's feelings and perceived failings. I demanded more and more. This eventually included not only others, but myself as well. I could always talk myself into one more late night at the office.

"On rare occasions I caught a glimpse in the mirror of what was happening," Michael continued, "and I didn't like what I saw. Rather than deal with it, I put the mirror in a box, locked it up, and became defensive if anybody suggested I look inside. That's why when your calls reminded me of what was going on, I found some reason to cut the conversations short. When you eventually, and with good cause, stopped trying to break through, I felt relieved of some pressure, but in another way sad and even more alone."

"I'm sorry," said the Professor. "We know we let you down."

"Don't beat yourself up about it. I was a hard nut to crack," replied Michael, "and I made it damn rough. To make a long story short, I became an all too willing victim of my own ego. As you said, it became all about serving me instead of serving Him."

"I know that this has been a painful journey for you," said the Minister, "but from what you have just told us, it sounds like you have come through it with a changed heart."

"I hope so," said Michael. "I feel blessed that I may have a second chance to be a new kind of man. I want to show my gratitude to God by serving as a leader in a way that would make Jesus smile with pride."

"This has been quite a night," said the Minister, "and without pushing the sailboat analogy too far, I'd say that you've had the barnacles scraped off your heart and are ready for the next phase of this prelaunch inspection, which I suggest we take up in the morning."

"Sounds good," Michael said wearily. "And thanks again for letting me bend your ears like this."

"No problem," said the Professor, rousing himself from his chair to give Michael a big hug. "I only wish we could have caught up with you sooner. But we have you now, and we're not going to let you go it alone again."

Before going to bed, the Minister led them in a prayer of gratitude for God's mercy and grace, asking for wisdom to see how they could better serve him.

16

Clearing the Head

The next morning the weather turned cold, and a light intermittent rain began to fall. Michael slipped out quietly in his all-weather running gear to do his morning run. It had become an automatic part of his daily routine ever since the doctor cleared him to start exercising again.

The Minister, after beginning his day as he always did—on his knees in prayer—started breakfast and lighted what promised to be an all-day fire in the fireplace.

The Professor slept in, enjoying the heavy camp blankets and the sound of the rain, until the smell of coffee and the cracking of the fire teased him into wakefulness.

As the three men settled in front of the fire after a leisurely breakfast, the Minister turned to Michael.

"Before we move on with our prelaunch checklist, it might be helpful to remind ourselves about the dangers of pride and an ego-filled heart—reminders that will keep you in good shape as you again serve as a leader."

"I'm all ears," Michael said.

"Okay," said the Minister. "One: An ego-filled heart always separates. It separates us from God, from each other, and from ourselves.

"Two: An ego-filled heart always compares. It's never satisfied, and it finds no peace in what it already has if someone else has more.

"Three: An ego-filled heart always deceives. It drives us to arrogance, complacency, and fear, all with equal force.

"There are two Bible verses that you may want to memorize to help prevent pride barnacles from attaching themselves to your heart. In Matthew 16:26 Jesus asked, 'What good will it be for a man if he gains the whole world, yet forfeits his soul?' The other verse is Romans 12:3—'Do not think of yourself more highly than you ought, but rather think of yourself with sober judgment, in accordance with the measure of faith God has given you.' "

"Good advice," responded Michael. "I certainly lost touch with my soul, and I don't want to let that happen again."

"We don't, either," said the Minister. "So let's move on to the next area of your prelaunch checkup: your rudder and steering mechanism."

"His what?" asked the Professor.

"His rudder and steering mechanism," replied the Minister with a smile.

"Just as I thought," said the Professor. "I knew all this sailing stuff would get us into trouble. What are you talking about—in plain language?"

"Bear with me now," said the Minister. "You'll see where I'm going in just a minute. Let me ask you: What role do you think the rudder and the steering mechanism play on a sailboat?"

"Well, Captain," the Professor answered jokingly, "I suppose they let you get where you want to go."

"Excellent," said the Minister. "And what do you think would happen if they were weakly constructed or poorly maintained?"

Michael interjected, "You would probably get into trouble when the going got rough, and never get where you were headed."

"Just like this conversation," said the Professor with a chuckle as he turned to the Minister. "I'm starting to get seasick. Don't keep us in suspense any longer."

"All right," replied the Minister. "What are Michael's rudder and steering mechanism?"

"I think I know the answer," Michael offered. "They're the principles, values, and concepts that I use as a leader to guide the direction of my organization."

"You've got it!" the Minister exclaimed.

"Thank goodness we're back on dry land," put in the Professor.

"I think your analogy is a good description of how I got into trouble," Michael said. "My rudder and steering mechanism were in bad shape. I didn't develop amnesia after the Baxter Center project and forget all the things I learned from the two of you, but I was so wrapped up in my own importance that I let the principles of good leadership take a back seat to my ego trip."

"Looking to the future," the Professor asked, "do you think you have the 'head' part of effective leadership sorted out and in place?"

"Not as well as the 'heart,' " Michael answered. "It wouldn't hurt to have a little refresher course on the method side of leadership."

17
Leadership Begins with a Clear Vision

"If I can rekindle my servant heart with your help," Michael continued, "what are the key leadership concepts that you believe are aligned with Jesus' method of servant leadership?"

Then, turning to the Professor, he said, "It's been almost five years since we've worked together. I'm sure some of your thinking has changed."

"And improved, I hope," said the Professor, laughing.

"I'm sure it has." Michael smiled. "Let's suppose you only had an hour to spend with a leader with a servant heart. What would you like to teach that person about leadership methods? I don't need to know everything—just some key concepts that will get the results I want and make Jesus proud."

"Good assignment!" said the Professor. "But before I begin, I want to clear up some misconceptions about servant leadership."

"Misconceptions?" wondered the Minister.

"Yes," responded the Professor. "In recent years, when I've talked to top managers about servant leadership, I sensed some real resistance to the concept."

"Why?" asked Michael.

"They assumed," said the Professor, "that servant leadership meant that they should work for their people and that their people would decide not only how to do their jobs but what their jobs were and when and how they should be done. To them, servant leadership sounded like the inmates would be running the prison."

"They were probably, just like I was, worried that servant leadership was about pleasing everyone," said Michael. "How did you answer their concerns?"

"I had to think fast," the Professor said, laughing. "All kidding aside, I was actually prepared. Since we worked with you, I have been doing a lot of soul-searching. In the process it became clear to me that there are two aspects of leadership—a visionary part and an implementation part."

"Don't some people say that leadership is really the visionary role and management is the implementation role?" asked Michael.

"Yes," said the Professor. "But I've come to think the leadership versus management debate is unproductive. I consider both the visionary role—'doing the right thing'—and the implementation role—'doing things right'—as leadership roles."

"Having a vision is important," said the Minister. "It's a picture of the future that produces passion in the leader, and it's this passion that people want to follow. The Bible says, 'Where there is no revelation, the people cast off restraint.' In other words, without guidance from God, law and order disappear. Without vision, the people perish."

"As a leader, if you cut people loose without any direction or guidelines, they'll be lost and the organization will suffer immeasurably," said the Professor. "Guidelines are boundaries. They channel energy in a certain direction. It's like a river. If you took away the banks, it wouldn't be a river anymore. Its momentum and direction would be gone. What keeps the river flowing is the banks."

"Remind me of the kind of boundaries people need for their energy to have direction and impact," said Michael.

"A clear vision has four aspects: purpose, values, image, and goals," replied the Professor.

"Please tell me more," said Michael.

"*Purpose* tells you what business you're in. It defines the fundamental reasons why you exist as an organization. *Values* determine how people should behave when they're working on the purpose," explained the Professor. "*Image* is really just a picture of what things would be like if everything were running as planned. And *goals* focus people's energy right now."

"In many ways I did all four of those at Baxter," said Michael.

"You sure did," said the Professor.

"I remember during my first week at the Baxter Center I met with all of the eight hundred employees in several groups. At each meeting I set the purpose, values, image, and 'big-picture' goals. I think I still have a card with it all written down."

With that, Michael reached into his pocket and pulled out his wallet. It didn't take him long to find one of his old Baxter cards. Then he looked up. "I always saved this for sentimental reasons. Unfortunately, I haven't looked at it for several years."

Then, reading from the card, he said:

Purpose: To create a city center that offers our community the best variety and quality of shopping, eating, and entertainment opportunities.

Operating Values:

ETHICAL—doing the right thing.

RELATIONSHIPS—raving-fan customers, gung-ho employees, satisfied owners, cooperative and pleased suppliers, and supportive community.

SUCCESS—establishing a well-run profitable organization.

Image: We want to be the best city center in the country. When people start thinking of urban revitalization, they'll think of the Baxter Center. People will be flying in from all over the country to find out how we do it.

"Everyone carried those little Baxter business cards with pride," said the Professor.

"They really did, didn't they?" said Michael, smiling.

"There was no mention about your goals on the card," wondered the Professor. "And I know you realize that all *good performance starts with clear goals.*"

"You certainly beat that into him," said the Minister, laughing.

"At the end of each meeting I began to deal with big-picture goals when I asked everyone to sign a pledge card that read:

" 'We the people of the Baxter Center are committed to be the best—the standard by which this industry is judged.'

"Then I asked all our people to come forward, one by one, with their signed pledges. As they handed them to me, I pinned a boomerang on their outfit. When everyone asked, 'Why a boomerang?' I was quick to answer, 'When you throw a boomerang, what does it do?'

"Everyone shouted, 'It comes back.'

" 'Those are our big-picture goals,' I told them. 'We're committed to be the best—the standard by which this industry is judged—*and* we want everyone to come back.' "

"I think you did a great job of setting up the vision and the banks for the Baxter project," said the Professor. "All great organizations have a visionary leader at the top who maintains a clear picture of the kind of organization it's going to be. People are inspired by vision. Once they understand the vision, they can begin to move toward it and even inspire others."

"I remember when we first talked about this aspect of leadership and the importance of establishing a clear vision," said the Minister to the Professor. "That was when I came to my initial realization that besides character, there was a 'method side' to effective leadership."

"Both are essential," reminded the Professor.

"That's for sure," said the Minister. "The more I thought, the more aware I became of how little credit I'd given Jesus as a practical teacher of leadership methods. It also became clear to me then that there was a great deal of compatibility between what you were teaching and how Jesus had trained and interacted with his disciples."

"It's been a while. Could you give us some examples?" said Michael.

"Sure," said the Minister. "When Jesus recruited his first disciples, Simon Peter and his brother Andrew, who were fishermen, he said, 'Come, follow me and I will make you fishers of men.' "

"That's interesting," said the Professor. "So Jesus, right from the beginning, began to instill in his disciples a greater purpose than just being fishermen."

"It certainly seems like it," said the Minister. "When I thought about the importance of passion in a vision, I immediately remembered Jesus saying:

" '. . . I have come that they may have life, and have it to the full.'

". . . have it to the full," repeated the Minister. "Giving life was Jesus' passion. He envisioned a world where people took the higher road—one of love and truth."

"Were love and truth the most important values for Jesus?" asked Michael.

"When it came to values," the Minister responded, "those two values, according to the Bible, seem to rise above all the rest:

> "And now these three remain: faith, hope, and love. But the greatest of these is love.

"When it came to truth, Jesus said it well: 'Then you will know the truth, and the truth will set you free.' "

"What was Jesus' big-picture goal?" wondered Michael.

"At the end of Jesus' ministry, he left his disciples with one huge goal:

> "Therefore go and make disciples of all nations, baptizing them in the name of the Father and of the Son and of the Holy Spirit, and teaching them to obey everything I have commanded you."

"That is a big-picture goal," said Michael.

"I can see now why people wanted to follow Jesus," said the Professor. "He provided them with clear direction and hope for this life and the next."

"And his Father provided direction for him." The Minister smiled.

"Precisely," said the Professor. "So establishing direction is the visionary aspect of leadership. And for that leadership function, the traditional hierarchical pyramid can stay upright."

"Stay upright?" asked Michael.

"Yes. Most organizations have a hierarchy that is pyramidal in nature," said the Professor. "I would imagine your present company does, too. Who's at the top of your hierarchy? You?"

Turning to the Minister, Michael said, "I'm sure you would say Jesus is, but I'm the president. I report to a board of directors. They hired me and they can fire me."

"Who's at the bottom of your official hierarchy?" asked the Minister.

"I guess our staff is—the folks who have the most day-to-day interaction with our customers. Is there something wrong with that?"

"No, not necessarily, as long as you know what the traditional hierarchy is good for and also when it becomes less effective," said the Professor.

Then he asked the Minister with a twinkle in his eye, "Did Moses go up on the mountain with a committee to get the commandments?"

"Of course not," said the Minister, laughing, "otherwise he might never have come down."

"Or maybe he would have come down with three commandments and seven suggestions," said the Professor, smiling. "People look to their leaders for vision and direction, so the traditional hierarchy is effective for this part of leadership. While you want to involve your experienced people in shaping the direction, as a leader you can't delegate this function. The responsibility for establishing vision and direction falls to you."

"What about the implementation part of leadership?" asked Michael.

"Why don't we take a break and save that for after lunch," suggested the Professor.

"Good idea," said Michael. "My circuits are already dangerously overloaded with information."

"So are mine," chimed in the Minister.

18

If You Want Your People to Be Responsible, You Must Be Responsive

After lunch, the Professor rekindled the fire while the Minister and Michael made themselves comfortable.

"Okay," said Michael. "Let's get to the real action—implementation."

"Implementation is where most organizations and leaders get in trouble," the Professor began. "The traditional pyramid-like hierarchy is kept alive and well. When this happens, who do people think they work for? The person above them or below them?"

"Obviously the person above them," replied Michael. "Their boss."

"Right!" said the Professor, as he sketched a diagram on his pad to show the others.

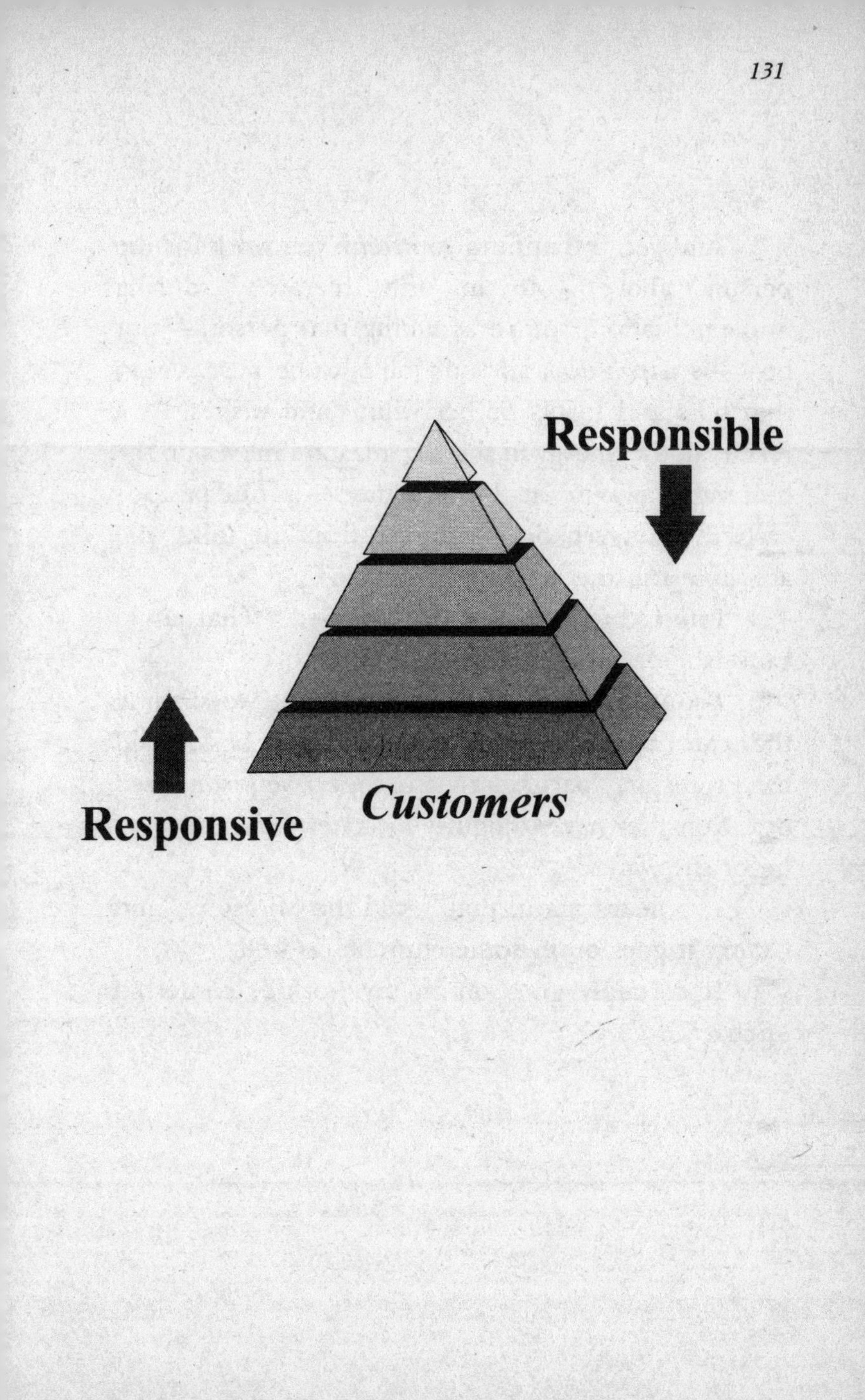
Responsible
Responsive
Customers

"And yet, the minute you think you work for the person above you in the hierarchy during implementation, you're assuming that person—your boss—is *responsible* and your job is to be *responsive* to that boss and to his or her whims and wishes. As a result, all the energy in the organization moves up the hierarchy, away from the customers—in our pastor's case, the congregation—and the frontline folks who are closest to the action."

"Interesting," mused the Minister. "That could cause some serious problems."

"People tell me all the time that the worst thing that can happen to them is to lose their boss," said the Professor, "particularly one they have just figured out. Now they have to figure out a new boss and what he or she wants."

"I've heard about that," said the Minister, "and I know it goes on in some churches as well."

"It certainly goes on in my world," confessed Michael.

"Unfortunately, it happens all the time in all sorts of organizations," said the Professor. "As a result, the most important people in organizations—those individuals who have contact with customers—spend all their time looking over their shoulders trying to figure out what their boss wants rather than focusing on the needs of the customer. They respond to customer requests like a duck."

"A duck?" questioned Michael.

"Yes," said the Professor. "There are two kinds of people in life: ducks and eagles. Ducks go 'Quack! Quack! Quack!' when any problem occurs, while eagles soar and take care of any problems."

"You run into a lot more ducks than eagles in organizations, don't you?" commented the Minister.

"You better believe it," answered Michael. "Unfortunately, even in my own."

"Whenever a duck appears, you know that the traditional pyramid-like hierarchy is alive and well," said the Professor, laughing. "I just ran into one last week."

"Where?" wondered Michael.

"I was on a trip recently and got to my hotel about ten in the morning. When I went to check in, they told me to go to the tenth floor. My room was on the concierge floor and I could check in there. When I got to the tenth floor, I was greeted by a bright, energetic woman. She checked me in but said I couldn't get into my room until after 2:00 P.M. because they had been full the night before. That wasn't any problem for me. She offered to keep my bags and have them put in my room when it was ready. Everything was going well until she said, 'Can I do anything else for you?'

" 'Yes,' I said. 'I need to cash a traveler's check.'

" 'Oh, no,' she said. 'I can't do that.' (Quack! Quack!)

" 'Why not?' I asked.

" 'I don't have your room number.' (Quack! Quack!)

" 'What do you mean?'

" 'I have to write down the room number on every check.' (Quack! Quack!) 'And I don't know your room number yet.'

" 'But you have my bags,' I said.

" 'I know, but it's our policy,' she moaned (Quack! Quack!).

" 'It's a good policy,' I said, 'but it doesn't make sense if you have someone's bags.'

" 'I'm sorry, I just work here.' (Quack! Quack!) 'I don't make the policies.' (Quack! Quack!) 'Would you like to talk to my supervisor?' (Quack! Quack!)"

"So people end up defending policies rather than serving their customer," said the Minister.

"They certainly do," said the Professor, "because they think that's what their boss wants them to do. After all, they aren't paid to think."

"Ridiculous, isn't it?" said Michael.

"It sure is," agreed the Professor. "I used to get mad at those frontline folks until I realized it wasn't their fault. Who do you think this woman worked for—a duck or an eagle?"

"A duck." Michael smiled. "If she worked for an eagle, that kind of boss would eat the duck—train her or fire her."

"We call the supervisory duck the 'Head Mallard,' " said the Professor, laughing, "because he just quacks at a higher level. Who do you think the supervisory duck works for?"

"Another duck," said Michael.

"Who works for another duck; who works for another duck. And finally, who sits on the top of the hierarchy?"

"A huge duck," said Michael, laughing. "This would be really funny if it wasn't so sad. How do you correct this situation?"

"One way is by inverting the traditional pyramidal hierarchy and turning it upside-down when it comes to implementation, and giving your customer contact people responsibility."

"When you turn the hierarchy upside-down, who is now at the top of the organization?" asked the Minister.

"The customer contact people," answered the Professor. "Who really is at the top of the organization?"

"In my case, it's our customers," said Michael. "Does that mean I would be at the bottom of the hierarchy, then?"

"Exactly," said the Professor. "When you turn the hierarchy upside-down philosophically, who serves whom when it comes to implementation?"

"You serve your people," said Michael.

"As a leader, your people are your customers. This one change, while it seems minor, makes a major difference."

"I would imagine the difference is between who is responsible and who is responsive," said Michael.

"You've got it," said the Professor. "With the traditional hierarchy, the boss is always responsible and his or her people are supposed to be responsive to or serve the boss." The Professor quickly drew another diagram.

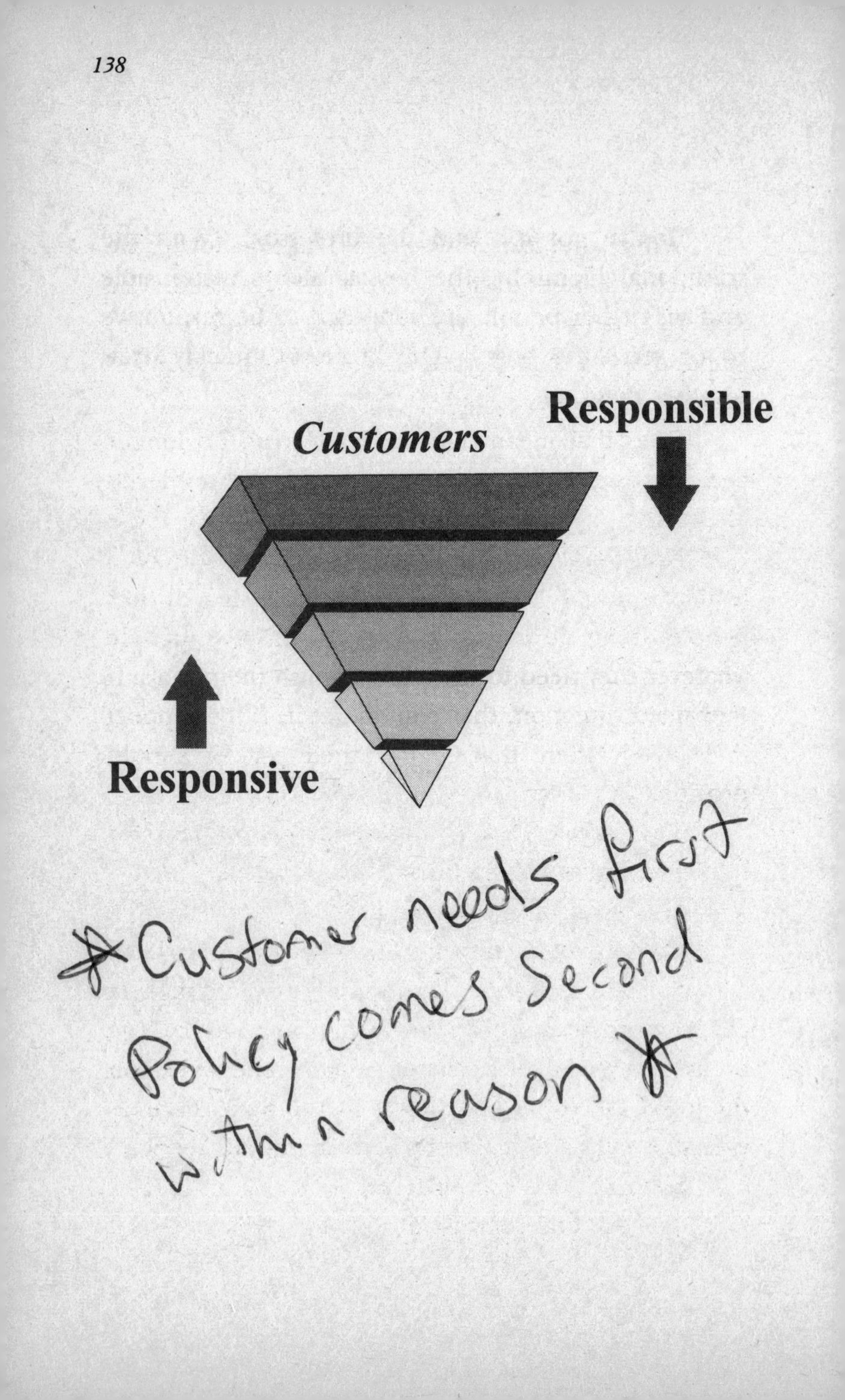
Customers
Responsible
Responsive
*Customer needs first
Policy comes second
within reason*

"When you turn the pyramid upside-down, the hierarchy changes and those roles get reversed. The leader's people become responsible—able to respond—and the job of the leader is to be responsive or serve his or her people."

"Does that mean that the leader can no longer be directive with his or her people?" wondered Michael.

"No!" said the Minister. "When the job of a leader is to be responsive or to serve his or her people, that means that leader will give people whatever they need to win—accomplish their goals. If they need direction, they should get it. If it's support they need, then that's what their leader should provide."

"That creates a very different environment for implementation, doesn't it?" Michael asked.

"Yes," said the Professor.

"Could you give me an example?" asked Michael.

"Sure," said the Professor. "My daughter experienced it recently during her summer college break at a great retail chain. After several weeks on the job, I asked her what it was like to work there, as everyone talks about the store's tremendous service.

"She said, 'It's very different.'

" 'What's different about it?'

" 'Well, the first thing that is different is their orientation program,' she said. 'Every employee has to go through a departmental orientation program before they can start work. The whole emphasis during the first part of the program is to teach everyone—all the associates—how to say, "No problem." The number one thing they want coming out of your mouth at their store is, "No problem." They want their people to be responsible.'

"Then I asked her, 'What else is different about working there?'

" 'My boss. About three or four times a day he comes up to me and asks, "Is there anything I can do for you?" He acts like he works for me.'

"The reality is that in great service companies like this one, the philosophy is that every manager works for his or her people. It's in relation to this responsive, serving role that the effective leader now encourages, supports, directs, coaches, facilitates, and does everything to help his or her people to soar like eagles and be successful. It's at this point," insisted the Professor, "where servant leadership really takes over. Now the leader is servant. Isn't that what Jesus did?"

"Yes," said the Minister. "It's interesting to reflect on history and recognize that all the great kings and queens sent their people out to die for them. Jesus was the only king who decided to die for his people."

"That's the ultimate in turning the hierarchy upside-down." Michael smiled.

"Yes," said the Minister. "In fact, when we talk about servant leadership, Jesus can serve as a model without even referring to his ultimate sacrifice."

"What do you know about Jesus as a leader?" the Professor asked Michael.

"Obviously not enough," said Michael, "but when we worked together I realized that Jesus was probably the only religious leader who built a leadership team."

"With twelve inexperienced people," said the Professor, laughing. "He could have recruited good preachers."

"You're right," said the Minister, smiling. "None of the disciples he chose had the kind of background that you would have expected him to need. In fact, some believe the only one who had any education was Judas."

"And he was the only turnover problem," kidded the Professor.

"You're right," said the Minister, "but Jesus built the remaining group into quite a team."

"For a long time I've been saying that *the important thing about being a leader is not what happens when you're there; it's what happens when you're not there,*" remarked the Professor. "You can usually get people to do what you want when you're there; the real test is what they do on their own. When Jesus was no longer physically present, his disciples seemed to carry on quite successfully. How did he make that happen?"

"He modeled servant leadership. Jesus was continually asked questions like, 'How do I become first?' Or, 'Who's the greatest?' " said the Minister. "His responses were consistent. In the Gospel of Mark he told his disciples:

> " 'If anyone wants to be first, he must be the very last and the servant of all.'

"And in the Gospel of Luke he said:

> " 'For he who is the least among you all—he is the greatest.'

"In light of the radical nature of what he was teaching them," said the Minister, "it was vital that Jesus make his answers clear to his disciples by both what he said and did.

"As recorded in the book of John, when Jesus washed the feet of the disciples," continued the Minister, "he demonstrated the true essence of servant leadership.

"When he'd finished washing their feet, he put on his garments and returned to his place and said:

> " 'Do you understand what I have done for you? . . . You call me "Teacher" and "Lord," and rightly so, for that is what I am. Now that I, your Lord and Teacher, have washed your feet, you also should wash one another's feet. I have set you an example that you should do as I have done for you. I tell you the truth, no servant is greater than his master, nor is a messenger greater than the one who sent him. Now that you know these things, you will be blessed if you do them.' "

"What an experience that must have been to have their Lord and Teacher humble himself and perform such a personal and intimate service," said Michael.

"Yes, it must have been quite an experience," said the Minister.

"While Jesus taught his disciples to be servants of all, he didn't send them out to serve without clear direction, did he?" inquired the Professor.

"Absolutely not," said the Minister.

"And he received his direction literally from the top of the hierarchy," said the Professor, smiling.

"You've got that right," said the Minister. "Once he revealed the vision of the Kingdom of God and how people could receive the grace of salvation, Jesus sent his disciples out to—in your terms—support, direct, encourage, coach, and facilitate other people to make the necessary choice."

"In other words," said Michael, "the spirit of servant leadership symbolized by the washing of the disciples' feet became operational only after the vision and direction were made clear."

"When you talk about being a servant leader in organizations, I'm sure you don't suggest that the leaders die for their people, do you?" said the Minister, smiling.

"Not in a physical sense," said the Professor, "but I certainly want them to be willing to voluntarily sacrifice some of their time and effort to listen to their people, to praise and encourage them and help them win."

"Is there anything else you would teach leaders?" asked Michael.

"Yes," said the Professor. "I think one of the functions servant leaders have to fulfill is that of being performance coaches. But why don't we hold that until after dinner. Right now I'm on overload and could use some time to relax."

"That sounds good to me," said Michael. "It's fabulous to be with you two again. I can't tell you how much I appreciate your love, concern, and the time you have sacrificed for both Carla and me."

"I don't care what anyone says, I think you're okay," said the Minister, smiling.

"God bless you, too." Michael laughed.

19

The Servant Leader as a Performance Coach

After dinner, the three men decided to take a walk. It was a beautiful evening, and the lake was aglow from the reflection of the setting sun.

"So tell me about the performance coaching aspect of leadership," said Michael.

"It might be the best answer to people who think servant leadership means trying to please everyone, as you did, Michael," the Professor began.

"Let me start by reviewing some of my past thinking on the subject. I used to proclaim that *people who feel good about themselves produce good results.*"

"Isn't that true?" questioned the Minister.

"It is," said the Professor, "but after a while I realized that maybe I'd been caught up in the old human relations game. You see, you can put too much emphasis on people feeling good about themselves without regard to performance. When that happens you might get high morale but low performance. You want both.

"So I changed that saying around to *people who produce good results feel good about themselves*. To me, the main function of servant leaders," insisted the Professor, "is to help their people produce good results by modeling and encouraging the behaviors and values that are aligned with a shared vision. When that happens, the organization wins and the people feel good about themselves."

"How do you make that happen?" asked Michael.

"Let me refer back to my ten years of college teaching. It seemed like I was always in trouble. In fact, I was investigated by some of the best faculty committees. The thing that most drove the faculty crazy was that I always gave out the final exam questions to my students on the first day of class."

"Really?" exclaimed Michael.

"The faculty responded the same way you just did," said the Professor. "They would ask me, 'What the heck are you doing?'

"I'd say, 'I'm confused.'

"They'd say, 'You act it.'

"I'd respond, 'I thought we were supposed to teach these students.'

" 'You are,' they'd say, 'but don't give the students the questions to the final exam.'

"I'd reply, 'Not only am I going to give them the final exam questions, but what do you think I'm going to do all semester? I'm going to teach them the answers so when it comes time for the final exam, they'll get A's.' "

"Were you considered an easy grader?" asked the Minister.

"I was by the faculty, but the students felt I really pushed them, because the exams weren't easy. I've discovered that people don't mind tough goals if they know they have a manager who's in their corner."

"Aren't most managers in their people's corners?" asked Michael.

"Not unless they're servant leaders," answered the Professor. "You see, there are three parts to an effective performance management system: performance planning, day-to-day coaching, and performance evaluation."

"What do you do during the performance planning stage?" asked the Minister.

"That's where you set the goals. Remember, all good performance starts with clear goals."

"I got that." Michael smiled.

"In my teaching example, giving the students the final exam on the first day of class is performance planning," said the Professor.

"Well, they certainly knew what the goals were for the semester," commented the Minister.

"Exactly," said the Professor. "Day-to-day coaching involves observing your people's performance, praising progress, and redirecting efforts that are off-base. Teaching the students the answers corresponds to this component."

"I imagine administering the actual final exam at the end of the semester parallels performance evaluation," said Michael.

"Right," said the Professor. "Which of these three activities—performance planning, day-to-day coaching, or performance evaluation—do you think gets the most attention and effort by most managers?" asked the Professor.

"I'd guess performance evaluation," replied Michael.

"Unfortunately, that's the truth. When I visit organization after organization and ask about their performance review system, they show me their evaluation forms. I usually tell them they can throw most of the forms out."

"Why?" wondered Michael.

"Those forms usually measure ridiculous things like 'willingness to take responsibility,' 'initiative,' 'promotability'—and these things are very difficult to judge and the judgments are entirely subjective. As a result, everyone is 'buttering up' the hierarchy—trying to please the boss and be liked by him or her. The traditional top-down hierarchy is alive and well."

"I meant to talk to you about that," responded Michael. "Where does the hierarchy fit in here?"

"When it comes to performance planning, the traditional pyramid-like hierarchy should stay upright," said the Professor. "In other words, leaders at all levels represent the organizational goals, and therefore should have a major input on individual goals."

"Does that mean people don't get involved in goal-setting?" asked Michael. "Do their leaders just tell them what their goals are?"

"Absolutely not, especially if they're servant leaders," said the Professor. "And the more experienced people are, the more involved in goal-setting they get. But the impetus has to come from the servant leader. When it comes to day-to-day coaching, now the hierarchy starts to turn upside-down and servant leaders begin to work for their people. At that point the goals are clear and now a servant leader's main focus is helping people accomplish their goals."

"Don't some organizations do a good job of performance planning?" asked Michael. "I know ours does—all our managers set goals with their people."

"You'd be surprised how few organizations do that," replied the Professor. "But even in organizations where managers sit down with their people and agree upon goals and objectives, after that is done, these goals often get filed away and forgotten until the end of the year, when managers are told to evaluate their people's performance."

"That hits home with me," said Michael. "At the end of the fiscal year there's always a frantic search for the established goals so the managers can complete evaluation forms on their people."

"That's an environment where it's difficult to be a servant leader," continued the Professor.

"Why?" wondered Michael.

"Because day-to-day coaching is the least used component of the three-part performance management system," said the Professor. "And yet, coaching is the most important servant leadership element in helping people accomplish their goals. Once goals are clear, servant-hearted leaders should wander around and 'teach people the answers,' so when these people get to the final exam most of them get A's. After all, for servant leaders, life is all about helping people get A's. They want their people to win. They aren't threatened by people around them who perform well."

"What I'd like to hear," said Michael, "is how you help people get A's. In other words, how you take *potential winners* and make them winners."

"As a servant leader, if you want to help potential winners perform well in a particular task regardless of whether you're around or not—there are five steps," said the Professor.

"First, you have to *tell them what to do.* Second, you have to *show them what to do.*"

"It makes sense that inexperienced people need direction?"

"Yes. They're usually enthusiastic about the job given them, but don't have a clue about what to do or how to do it. If you delegate responsibility and leave them alone, they will fail."

"I imagine that happens a lot," said the Minister.

"Yes it does. That's why the next two steps are very important.

"The third step is to *let them try* what you want them to do. And the fourth step is to *observe their performance.* It's this fourth step that's forgotten the most. Some managers are good at telling and showing people what to do. Then they disappear, only to return when there's a problem. That's what we call seagull management."

Michael smiled. "Seagull management?"

"Yes," said the Professor. "Seagull managers aren't around until there's a problem. Then they fly in, make a lot of noise, dump on everybody, and then fly out."

"Not a fun way to be managed," said the Minister. "And certainly not a servant leadership approach."

"That's why that fourth step—*observing*—is all-important for servant leaders in developing potential winners. It sets up the fifth step, which is to *praise progress or redirect.* This is where you're giving the real coaching and support. The key to developing people is to catch them doing something right—in the beginning, approximately right. Praise progress, it's a moving target."

"That's novel," said Michael. "In most organizations, managers spend all their time catching people doing things wrong."

"I know," said the Professor. "And that's why people get discouraged. The key to developing people is to accent the positive. Servant leaders know that."

"What if people are doing something wrong?"

"Then, as a servant leader, you redirect them, and go back to show and tell and start the process all over again. If you work closely with people in the beginning and they start to develop, after a while they can begin to provide their own direction and support, and you can supervise them less."

"That's exactly what Jesus did with his disciples," said the Minister. "He modified his approach with them as they progressed from being inexperienced in what he wanted them to do—be fishers of men—until the point when they were able to carry on without his physical presence."

"That's interesting," said the Professor.

"It sure is," said the Minister. "When Jesus first sent out the twelve two by two, he was certainly directing them." Opening the Bible, he said, "Let me read you his instructions to them:

> " 'Take nothing for the journey except a staff—no bread, no bag, no money in your belts. Wear sandals but not an extra tunic. Whenever you enter a house, stay there until you leave that town. And if any place will not welcome you or listen to you, shake the dust off your feet when you leave, as a testimony against them.'

"He gave these instructions early in his training of these men. Later, as we have talked about, at the end of the book of Matthew, Jesus has by now moved to the point where he's able to delegate to his disciples. He tells them:

> " 'All authority in heaven and on earth has been given to me. Therefore go and make disciples of all nations, baptizing them in the name of the Father and of the Son and of the Holy Spirit, and teaching them to obey everything I have commanded you.'

"He had authority and was delegating to them. But he was constantly coaching them all along the way, until he was no longer present on a day-to-day basis."

"Didn't you tell me once," Michael asked, "that Jesus told them he would be with them forever?"

"That's right," replied the Minister. "He said, 'And surely I am with you always, to the very end of the age.' A good servant leader is always available if he or she is needed. Jesus is there for us now if we're willing to get our egos out of the way, and ask for help."

Michael nodded. "So Jesus was a performance coach—and that's what I'm supposed to be, too."

"Absolutely," said the Professor. "That's the last key method you need to be an effective servant leader."

"If you rekindle your servant heart," said the Minister, "and combine it with these servant methods that the Professor described, I think you'll be on the right path."

"Talking about the right path," said Michael, "I think it's time for us to head back to the cabin. We're starting to lose the light."

As they walked quietly together, Michael broke the silence. "I guess my biggest concern in all this is losing the light. I know in my head what's right for me to do. But I'm still worried about whether I can keep my commitment and follow through."

"That gets at one last part of my sailboat analogy," said the Minister. "It has to do with your compass and navigation system—or to put it plainly, how you're going to keep on course when the weather gets rough."

"That's my issue," said Michael.

"Let's save that one for tomorrow morning," said the Professor. "It will be a great topic for ending our time together."

20
Guiding the Hands

The next morning the Minister suggested they walk to the village and continue their conversation over breakfast at a local lakeside restaurant that was famous for its blueberry pancakes.

After they had placed their order and settled in at the table, the Minister turned to Michael.

"I think I know what your concern is. Even if your heart is pure and your head is clear, what about your hands—your behavior?"

With that, the Minister wrote two words on a paper napkin: *Commitment* and *Follow-through.* Then he crossed the two words out.

"God knows you can't keep your commitment or follow-through," he continued. "We all fall short of perfection."

Then he wrote two new words on the napkin: *Accept* and *Trust.*

"What we need to do first is to accept the unconditional love that's available for us."

"That's hard for us mortals to do," Michael said.

"That's for sure. But it's a choice. Let me ask you both a question: Do you love your kids?"

Both Michael and the Professor smiled and nodded.

"Okay," said the Minister. "Then let me ask you both this: Is your love of your children dependent on their success? In other words, if they're successful you'll love them, but if they aren't, you won't?"

"Of course not," Michael answered. "I love my kids regardless of how successful they may be."

"I agree," said the Professor.

"Then you love your kids unconditionally?"

"I guess we do," Michael said.

The Minister continued, "Then why won't you accept that unconditional love for yourself? After all, God didn't make junk."

"I see what you're getting at," Michael said. "Our lives would be completely different if we accepted the unconditional love that's available to us every day."

"Right," said the Minister. "And then, if we trust Jesus as our forgiver, model, and guide, we have a chance to stay on track."

"Please tell us more," Michael said.

"Jesus modeled some wonderful habits of leadership—things he did to prepare and sustain himself throughout the trials and temptations of his daily walk as a leader," the Minister continued. "This is where the navigation analogy comes in. Jesus took time in all major crises of his ministry to make sure he stayed headed in the right direction. He did this by checking his spiritual compass through times of solitude and prayer. He continually recalibrated his activities against the true north of his Father's will. In doing so he showed us how to keep on course as we strive to be good leaders.

"Michael, I think the best advice I can give you and the biggest challenge for us all is to keep our eyes on Jesus—our spiritual true north—and spend time daily to ask him for direction and help.

"There's a story in the book of Mark that hit me right between the eyes when I reread it several months ago. It tells of a time early in Jesus' ministry when he'd been healing people and casting out demons well into the evening. People of the town gathered around the door of the house where he was staying."

Opening his Bible, the Minister said, "The text then tells us what happened the next day.

> "Very early in the morning, while it was still dark, Jesus got up, left the house and went off to a solitary place, where he prayed. Simon and his companions went to look for him, and when they found him, they exclaimed: 'Everyone is looking for you!'

"As you read this narrative," the Minister continued, "you can almost feel the excitement in the voices of those who went to find Jesus. They were ready for him to continue to please the crowd and to draw people to their cause through his miraculous healings.

"The answer Jesus gave them speaks to the point I'm trying to make. Jesus replied, 'Let us go somewhere else—to the nearby villages—so I can preach there also. That is why I have come.'

"Despite pressure to continue to work where he was well received, Jesus responded to a higher calling to go elsewhere. He chose the best use of his time and opportunities to stay on purpose rather than the good and the popular. This is the kind of discernment and steadiness of purpose that came after he'd sought to commune with God and renew his spiritual true north.

"Solitude, prayer, and the daily study of Scripture seem to be important ways for any of us to stay on track as we seek to lead others as God would have us lead them."

"I appreciate what you're saying," Michael said. "I know that when I went to New York, one of the first things that suffered in my daily routine was my time alone with God and my prayer life. I see now it was one of the major causes of my getting off-track. The less time I spent connecting with God and focusing on his vision and values, the more isolated I became, and the more my ego began to seek other ways to feel good."

"Understanding that is a major accomplishment, Michael," said the Minister.

"I hope so," said Michael.

"What are your goals as you head back into your leadership pressure cooker?" asked the Professor.

"I've thought a lot about it," said Michael. "I think I should have four goals at work if I'm going to focus on spiritual significance more than earthly success. I'd like to repeat them to you:

"First, to honor God in everything I do.

"Second, to help develop our people to their highest potential.

"Third, to pursue excellence in serving our customers.

"And fourth, to strive to grow profitably."

"Great goals," said the Minister. "I think the first two should be your 'end' goals, and the last your 'means' goals."

"Interesting twist," Michael said. "So the only reason to pursue excellence with customers or to grow profitably is to honor God and to develop more people to their highest potential."

"Amen!" said the Minister.

When they returned to the cottage, Michael and the Professor prepared to head to the airport for a pair of early-afternoon flights, while the Minister packed his car for the drive home.

At the Minister's suggestion, they spent the rest of the morning first in a time of prayer for their families and their new beginnings, and then in a time of solitude. In their solitude—by talking to God directly and listening for his answer—they sought to gain a new perspective on what he would have them do.

As the Professor and Michael said goodbye to the Minister, the three friends promised to pray for one another daily and to stay in touch regularly to keep each other on course. "A cord of three strands," the Minister reminded them, "is not quickly broken."

21

The Return of the Servant Leader

The first thing Michael did on the flight home was to take out the sheet the Minister had given him describing the twelve-step *FaithWalk* Leadership Program and to begin thinking through the first three steps. It was an act he would repeat many times in the days ahead as he attempted to walk the talk of servant leadership.

He was quick to admit to himself that on more than one occasion he had allowed his ego needs and his drive for earthly success to negatively impact his role as a leader. *My leadership certainly hasn't been like that of Jesus,* he thought.

However, as a result of his talks with the Minister and the Professor, Michael had come to believe that God could transform his leadership motives, thoughts, and actions into the servant leadership that Jesus modeled.

He decided that day to turn his leadership efforts over to God. In doing so, he committed to become an apprentice of Jesus and his servant leadership example.

The most difficult of the twelve steps for Michael to maintain was the fourth one, about making a searching, fearless inventory of his leadership motives, thoughts, and behaviors that were inconsistent with servant leadership. He realized from the very first that this would have to be an ongoing process. Being truthful with himself in this way, though not always easy, was absolutely essential as the foundation of his *FaithWalk* Leadership journey.

When he arrived home late that night, Michael was anxious to tell Carla all that had happened during his time with the Professor and the Minister. They stayed up talking until after two in the morning. Michael admitted to Carla that he'd come to realize how many times he had behaved in ways that did not make Jesus proud.

"But I'm ready to let go and let God," Michael said. "I've asked him to remove my shortcomings and strengthen me against the temptations of greed, recognition, and power."

Michael also asked for Carla's forgiveness for letting her down in the past. "From now on," he told her, "I want to keep my priorities in order: First comes God, then you, then the kids, and finally my job. If I do that, when something goes wrong at the office, I still have a lot left over. Before—when everything I did was focused on the outside—I was devastated by any setback at work, or whenever I didn't get my own way."

As Michael talked, Carla was hopeful but still apprehensive about what would happen after the "high" of the retreat wore off. But she was greatly encouraged when Michael told her about a conference call the three men had scheduled for the following morning.

"It's the first of our weekly accountability meetings," said Michael, smiling.

* * *

In the months that followed, the three friends talked every week. Often the Professor and the Minister were together on a speakerphone—it gave them special time together—and Michael was in his office in New York.

At the Professor's suggestion, their weekly meetings took on a specific format. They took turns opening their sessions with a short prayer—asking for guidance during the meeting from what the Minister liked to call the "great three-person consulting team": the Father, who had started the whole thing; the Son, who modeled it; and the Holy Spirit, who was the day-to-day coach.

Using the Bible as their textbook, they would then study character issues or methods of servant leadership that were of particular value in helping Michael with his fast-growing company.

Their discussion then turned to a short series of questions they had agreed to ask each other each time they met. Each question related to some character aspect or leadership method they were trying to integrate into their behavior. At first, they focused mainly on Michael's responses to the questions, but eventually all three men had a chance to be heard and helped. The questions weren't designed for open-heart surgery on each other, or to trigger unsolicited advice. What they provided was a method of mutual accountability and support for acting on their good intentions.

Strict confidentiality was the spoken and agreed-upon rule. Nothing left the table without the permission of all parties.

Each session, which usually lasted about ninety minutes, came to an end with each man asking for prayer in a particular area of leadership for the coming week.

As they shared their triumphs and failures and the soul-healing impact of laughter, the three men bonded together as never before. Whenever any of them faced a particularly tough situation, he could count on a call of support from the others precisely at the right time.

* * *

Michael took several positive steps on his journey back to proper balance in his life and servant leadership on the job when he returned to work. Even with the Minister and the Professor back on his team, Michael thought it would be good to have a local support group, too. So he telephoned the corporate manager he'd told Carla about before his heart attack—the one who impressed him by seeming to have her priorities in order—and talked to her about creating a fellowship/accountability group with two or three other top managers. She thought it was a good idea, and they committed themselves to make it happen.

Michael also developed three personalized lists of *Checkpoints* to remind him daily of what he was trying to do—to follow Jesus' leadership example as described in the Bible. He could refer to these lists anytime he felt himself getting off course.

CHECKPOINT 1

My Servant HEART—Leadership Character

1. *Effective leadership starts on the inside.*

   - Real change in behavior eventually requires a transformation of the heart. That's where the core of who I am resides.
   - Jesus' message was not just for the mind. It was directed at my heart. It was a real heart attack; it was about character change. Jesus is interested in me being a different person—a good and caring human being.

2. *True leadership starts on the inside with a servant heart, then moves outward to serve others.*

   - As a *servant first* and a leader second, I will assume leadership only if I see it as a way in which I can serve. I'm "called" to leadership, rather than driven to it, because I naturally want to be helpful.
   - Jesus did not want his disciples to be leaders first; he wanted them to become servants first. He told them:

> "*Not so with you.* Instead, whoever wants to be great among you must be your servant and whoever wants to be first must be slave to all."

3. *Leaders with servant hearts have certain characteristics and values in common:*

- My paramount aim is the best interest of those I lead.
- I gain personal satisfaction from watching the growth and development of those I lead.
- I have a loving care for those I lead.
- I want to be held accountable; I ask, "Has my performance met the needs of those I serve?"
- I'm willing to listen. In fact, I love feedback and advice—any information that will help me serve better.
- I have my ego under control. I don't think less of myself, I just think about myself less. I don't *E*dge *G*od *O*ut!

CHECKPOINT 2

My Servant HEAD—Leadership Methods

1. Leadership begins with a clear vision.

- There are two aspects of leadership—a visionary role (doing the right thing) and an implementation role (doing things right).
- A vision is a picture of the future that produces passion, and it's this passion that I and other people want to follow. An organization without clear vision is like a river without banks—it stagnates and goes nowhere.
- A clear vision has four aspects:
  Purpose—telling me and others what business we're in.
  Image—providing a picture of what things would be like if everything were running as planned.
  Values—determining how I and others should behave when working on the purpose.
  Goals—focusing my energy and the energy of others right now.

- The traditional pyramidal hierarchy is effective for the visionary aspect of leadership. People look to me as their leader for vision and direction. While I should involve experienced people in shaping direction, I can't and won't delegate the responsibility for establishing vision and direction.

2. *If I want people to be responsible, I must be responsive.*

- The implementation role—living according to the vision and direction—is where most leaders and organizations get in trouble. The traditional pyramid is kept alive and well, leaving the customers uncared for at the bottom of the hierarchy. All the energy in the organization moves up the hierarchy as people try to please and be responsive to their boss, leaving the customer contact people—those closest to the customer—to be "ducks," quacking away: "It's our policy," "I just work here," or "Do you want to talk to my boss?"

- Effective implementation requires turning the traditional hierarchical pyramid upside-down so the customer contact people are at the top of the organization and can be responsible—able to respond and soar like eagles—while leaders like myself serve or are responsive to our people—helping them to accomplish goals and to live according to the vision and direction.
- The essence of servant leadership as symbolized by Jesus washing the feet of his disciples becomes operational only when the vision and direction are made clear to everyone.
- Clear vision comes first from the traditional hierarchy; implementation then follows with servant leadership, in which the shepherd is there for the benefit of the sheep.

3. The servant leader as a performance coach.

- There are three aspects of an effective performance management system:

Performance Planning—All good performance starts with clear goals.

Day-to-Day Coaching—Observing a person's performance, praising progress, and redirecting efforts that are off-base.

Performance Evaluation—Final assessment of a person's performance over a period of time.

- Most organizations emphasize performance evaluation, with some attention to performance planning. The area most often neglected is day-to-day coaching. *This is the most important area for servant leaders.* I focus my attention here.

- The five key steps for me, as a servant leader, to help potential winners become winners are:

  1. *tell them what to do.*
  2. *show them what to do.*
  3. *let them try.*
  4. *observe their performance, and then*
  5. *praise their progress, or redirect.*

- The step that's most often missed is observing performance. When I stop noticing performance, I have stopped being a performance coach. After Jesus gave his disciples the great commission, he told them he would be with them forever. He is always there ready to help. All servant leaders should do the same.

- My key to developing people is to catch them doing something right. In the beginning, when they're learning something new, it can be approximately right. I praise progress. I know it's a moving target.

CHECKPOINT 3

Servant HANDS—Leadership Behavior

1. *Servant leadership is not about pleasing everyone.*

    - I want to serve and help people to accomplish their goals and be effective, but my emphasis is on obedience to a higher mission and set of values.
    - Jesus certainly did not try to please everyone. His simple concern was to please God.
    - Servant leadership without a relationship to God can lead to an ego trip. E.G.O. = *E*dging *G*od *O*ut.

2. *Servant leaders focus on spiritual significance more than earthly success.*

    - I'm more concerned about generosity than accumulation of wealth.
    - I'm more concerned about service than recognition.
    - I'm more concerned about developing loving relationships than power and status.

- When I focus on spiritual significance, fulfilling earthly success can then follow.

3. *Effective servant leaders develop a triple bottom line.*

- I emphasize that profit is the applause we get by serving our customers well and providing a motivating and empowering environment for our people.

- All three factors—financial strength, raving-fan customers, and gung ho people—are important. If one is overemphasized at the expense of the others, our long-term effectiveness is limited.

4. *On a daily basis, effective servant leaders recalibrate their commitment to serve.*

- I have a support/accountability group to keep me on track.

- I make frequent use of the three disciplines: solitude, prayer, and the study of Scripture.

- I work my way through the twelve steps to *FaithWalk* Leadership:

1. I admit that on more than one occasion I have allowed my ego needs and drive for earthly success to impact my role as a leader.
2. I've come to believe that God can transform my leadership motives, thoughts, and actions.
3. I've made a decision to turn my leadership efforts over to God, and to become an apprentice of Jesus.
4. I make a daily inventory of my leadership motives, thoughts, and behaviors that are inconsistent with servant leadership.
5. I admit to God, to myself, and to my significant others the exact nature of my leadership gaps—when I behave in ways that do not make Jesus proud.
6. I am entirely ready to have God remove all character defects that have created gaps in my leadership.
7. I humbly ask God to remove my shortcomings and to strengthen me against the temptations of recognition, power, and greed.

8. I'm making a list of people whom I may have harmed by my ego-driven leadership, and I am willing to make amends to them all.
9. I make direct amends to each person whenever possible, unless doing so would injure them or others.
10. I continue to take personal inventory regarding my leadership role, and when I am wrong, I promptly admit it.
11. By engaging the disciplines of solitude, prayer, and study of the Scripture, I seek to align my servant leadership efforts with what Jesus modeled, and to constantly seek ways to be a servant first and a leader second with the people I encounter in my leadership responsibilities.
12. Having had a "heart attack" regarding the principles of servant leadership, I have tried to carry this message to other leaders, and to practice them in all my affairs.

When Michael returned to work, he found his company still performing well on the bottom line, but not functioning as a human organization in a way that mirrored his new thinking. Customer complaints were widespread, internal conflict was a way of life, and turnover was high, particularly among good people who could easily go elsewhere. An overemphasis on financial numbers was an invitation to long-term problems.

Michael was determined to turn that situation around and develop a solid triple bottom line that would turn his organization into what some called a "Fortunate 500" company. To keep that vision in mind, Michael put a plaque on his desk that read: *Profit is the applause you get for taking care of your customers and creating a motivating environment for your people.*

He quickly began the process of setting a clear vision with his key staff, while gathering feedback and suggestions from all levels of the organization. Everyone agreed that their purpose was to be the number one service provider in each of their businesses. They wanted to be the best and to set the standard in their industry. Integrity, commitment, and success were their three key values.

Michael conveyed constantly to everybody the company's desired image:

> We're going to be the best, not because we have the best prices or products—those are an entry requirement for running a successful business—but because we're the best at moments of truth: any moment when external or internal customers come in contact with somebody in our organization in a way that they could get an impression.

Satisfying customers was not the goal. The "big-picture goal" was creating *raving fans* out of them—customers so excited about the way they were treated that they wanted to brag about the company and its service. In many ways, these customers would become like salespeople for the company.

Michael knew from his work with the Professor and Minister that creating raving-fan customers would happen only if the people serving them were *gung ho*—if they knew that what they were doing was worthwhile, if they had control over achieving their goals, and if the leadership throughout the organization was cheering them on.

To make this happen, Michael immediately established a 360-degree feedback process so everyone could learn how to serve others better. The new organizational chart, an inverted pyramid, was prominently displayed throughout the company. It was clear that the customer contact frontline people were at the top of the organization when it came to implementing the vision.

Michael met with all the key managers every Monday morning at eight for an hour. The first agenda item was always a praising barrage. People gave each other "thumbs up" and "high fives" for the help they had received or given. The last item of business at each meeting was having everyone say what they were doing that week and what help they might need.

The toughest thing Michael attempted to implement was to "walk their talk" and manage by their values. Since he knew that talking about God and Jesus as a model for leadership might turn a number of people off, he had to find another way to soften the hearts of leaders at every level of the organization.

Once the organization's purpose and values were established and behaviorally defined, they were communicated widely on business cards, brochures, annual reports, and framed posters in every work area. That was the easy part of managing by their values. The real challenge was aligning leadership behavior and organizational practices with the values. If the values were to be the boss, everyone had to be held accountable for adhering to them. Whenever there was a gap—an incident where a value was not followed—attention was focused on that incident, with the goal of making sure the misalignment never occurred again.

When the process started, all eyes were on Michael. Everyone expected that the old top management philosophy of "Do what I say, not what I do" would be alive and well. Michael knew that this philosophy typically prevails with managers who are leaders first and who keep the hierarchy upright for implementation, requiring all the energy to flow away from the customers up the hierarchy to top management. Michael wanted to break that pattern. He was committed to view feedback as a gift, so he could walk his talk.

Michael realized that leading as Jesus would have him lead, according to a set of values, makes a leader very vulnerable. He heard one top manager liken the process to "taking your clothes off in Times Square every day at noon." But Michael and his team stayed committed to aligning their behavior with the organization's values.

Positive results didn't happen all at once. Reestablishing trust wasn't easy. Michael faced great temptations to go for the quick fix when he became impatient or discouraged by the slow, but steady, pace of change. His ego, integrity, and personal confidence were challenged daily by both the applause and the criticism he received. Michael had to admit that as he sought to follow the guidance of Jesus and his servant heart, life hadn't gotten any easier—only better.

For meeting the pressures of his day, Michael found new strength and perspective to draw on from his daily time alone in prayer and meditation on the practical wisdom and inspiration of God's word. From God's gift of unconditional love that Michael now willingly received, he gained an internal peace that flowed into all his other relationships.

As for Carla and their children, the fear and insecurity caused by Michael's heart attack was replaced with a new sense of security and closeness as he regained his spiritual bearings.

The mutual support he shared with the Minister and the Professor and his local accountability group kept Michael from retreating into the isolation and compartmentalized lifestyle that had caused his earlier fall. As he continued engaging daily in honest self-assessment of his leadership, Michael found new joy and significance in his role as a servant leader.

And as he made honest attempts to align his own thoughts and behavior with Jesus as his model of servant leadership, and to recalibrate the vision and values he'd helped establish for the company, the people responded.

It was amazing to see the reenergized company. The bottom line—the profit—which had been good, got better. But unlike before, everyone in the organization was now excited about the company, and especially the encouragement that they received from Michael. He was seldom in his office, but instead was always around catching people doing things right and praising their progress. When something went wrong he never punished people, but redirected their efforts in the right direction. As Michael modeled this servant leadership behavior, his managers began to follow suit.

After a time, Michael was a hero not only to the stockholders, but also to the customers, the employees, his family, and the community. But this time it didn't go to his head. He kept things in proper perspective through his daily prayers and consistent focus on "What would Jesus do?" as well as his ongoing fellowship with Carla and the kids, with the Professor and the Minister, and with his local accountability group.

One evening, a year after he'd returned to work, Carla put her arms around Michael and whispered in his ear, "You know what, Michael, you've made me and Jesus smile with pride."

"I hope so," he replied. "But the real test might be ahead. I'm hearing rumblings about a possible hostile takeover of our company by a large multinational corporation that could put me and a number of my team out on the streets. It could dismantle much of what we've accomplished and the hopes of our people. The question is, Will I be able to trust God and help others to do the same—no matter what the future holds?"

EPILOGUE I

The Minister

The Minister was already deep in thought as he pulled out of the driveway to begin the familiar trip to church. It was his first day back from his sabbatical and his weekend with Michael and the Professor.

The time away from the pressures of the ministry had provided him with important new perspectives on his leadership. With renewed eagerness he was ready to serve the needs of the people God had entrusted to his care. He'd come to grips with his own limitations in attempting to please everyone and do everything himself. He felt his heart had been in the right place. But he had to admit his ego had clouded his decisions as he tried to live up to the image of the twenty-four-hour-a-day pastor-teacher.

Through extended time in prayer and reflection, he affirmed that his primary calling was to preach and inspire the spiritual growth of his congregation. The Minister was grateful that he'd been uniquely gifted to present the truth of God's love to followers of Jesus and those still seeking answers to life's important questions.

He knew it took time and energy to fulfill the vision-setting aspects of leadership. He was motivated now to find new ways to equip and empower his staff and lay leadership partners to implement the operational aspects of the ministry.

It was now a whimsical experience for the Minister when he read the Old Testament account of how Moses had to be coached by his father-in-law to stop trying to do everything himself and learn how to delegate. The Minister was strangely comforted that the first organizational issue the disciples had to face as a result of church growth required the same reassignment of day-to-day ministry functions that he would be called to implement.

His insight from the methods of leadership he learned from the Professor showed him how he had allowed his feelings of responsibility for everything that happened within the church to drain his energy and thwart the growth of his staff and lay leader partners. The Minister came to realize the latent power that could be released by developing the leadership competencies and empowerment of his staff and lay volunteers. By being responsive to their growth needs as they assumed greater autonomy and accountability, the Minister felt he would now be able to multiply the impact of his energies and values as a leader.

There was much to be done, but he knew he would not have to do it alone. As he made his way through the quiet streets of the early morning, the Minister was filled with renewed hope and assurance for leading his people. It sprang from his belief that as he continued his journey, daily seeking guidance and wisdom from Jesus, he would find the answers no matter what the question.

EPILOGUE II
The Professor

The line continued to move at its usual snail's pace as the Professor waited to board the early-morning flight to Chicago. By the end of the self-imposed ban he and Allison placed on business travel during the summer, the Professor, refreshed, looked forward to reentering the mainstream of the marketplace.

He would be on the road for two solid weeks with speaking engagements and visits to some of his corporate consulting clients. As he settled into his seat, listening with a disinterested ear to the flight attendant's preflight seat-buckle mantra, the Professor scanned his itinerary. It included meeting with several long-term fans of his books and management seminars, as well as speaking engagements that were bound to attract new audiences. It was to be a familiar routine, made interesting by the fact that the Professor was planning on delivering a message different from what his audiences were used to hearing. His experience with Michael and the Minister had revealed the full impact of character on effective servant leadership.

The next day, the Professor shared his personal mission statement with his audience.

"My mission," he said, "is *to be a loving teacher and example of simple truths that helps myself and others to awaken the presence of God in our lives.* The truths I want to share with you today in as loving a way as possible are not very flattering to the way most of us run our lives and our organizations. By focusing a harsh light on what drives a lot of what we think and do as leaders, I hope to begin the process of redirection and healing that will unleash the true power of people working together to produce the most good for themselves and the world around them.

"What has become clear to me is that the biggest negative addiction in the world today is automatically considering every situation from the point of view of 'What's in it for me?'

"When this ego-addiction invades the halls of power and influence," continued the Professor, "leaders think and behave as if the sheep are there to serve the needs of the Shepherd. What this looks like in practical terms is a one-way flow of money, power, and recognition up the hierarchy, away from the people who actually take care of the customers.

"You've heard about the 'head' of the department and the 'hired hands.' We don't even give 'hired hands' a head," the Professor said with a chuckle. "Some people are considered to have supervision, and others to be subordinates or 'subordinary.' Self-interest and self-preservation dominate when ego rather than service to others is the motivating force.

"What I want to convince you of today," continued the Professor, "is that we are called by a Caller to serve others—not ourselves—and that it's truly better to give than to receive.

"To do that, I'm going to focus on the character of leadership as well as the methods. Effective leadership and effective living start on the inside with who you are—your character—and later move outward to impact your behavior."

The Professor reminded his listeners about their calling and the Caller, just as he'd been doing each day with the people he moved among, wherever he was. At first he'd thought he might be overdoing it, but his conviction that his mission was to awaken the presence of God in the lives of his audience gave him a new boldness. He constantly challenged himself by asking himself, *Do I love them enough to tell them the best I know?*

He ended his presentation with the following story.

"A couple of years ago at the Special Olympics the nine finalists in the hundred-yard dash prepared for the start of the race. When the gun went off, these contestants with various disabilities headed down the track toward the finish line. Part way down the track, one of the competitors fell. He tried to get up, but fell again. He tried again, but without success. Finally he just lay on the track and began to sob.

"One by one the other eight contestants heard his sobbing and stopped. They all headed back toward their fallen competitor. When they got there they helped him up and all nine contestants held hands, walked down the track, and crossed the finish line together. The crowd couldn't believe it. They rose to their feet and gave a fifteen-minute standing ovation.

"These young people may have been disabled physically, but they were very advanced spiritually. They knew that we're called to serve others, not ourselves. Go and do the same. God Bless!"

With those final words the Professor waved to the audience. They immediately rose to their feet and gave him a similiar standing ovation.

As he left the auditorium, elated at the response of the audience, the Professor caught his ego about to take flight, and bowed his head in a silent prayer of thanks for having been called to serve. And then, with a thankful heart, he committed to:

*

Share
This
Message
With
Others

*

THE END

Acknowledgments

The thinking that went into this book was not limited to us. We have been blessed to learn from a number of outstanding thinkers.

We would like to publicly praise: **Dallas Willard** for his wonderful book *The Divine Conspiracy* and all he taught us about God's plan for us today. **Tom Marshall** for his brilliant book *Understanding Leadership* that taught us how Jesus made servant leadership come alive. **Robert Greenleaf** for his groundbreaking book *Servant Leadership* and clarifying the difference between a strong natural leader and a strong natural servant. **Bob Buford** for his friendship and support and the inspiration he provided from his book *Halftime*. **Bob Russell,** Senior Pastor at Southeastern Christian Church in Louisville, Kentucky, for his help on clarifying the difference between earthly success and spiritual significance. **Paul Hersey,** cocreator of *Situational Leadership®*, for his breakthrough thinking around leadership. **Spencer Johnson,** coauthor of *The One Minute Manager®*, for his creative thinking about managing people.

Bob Lorber, coauthor of *Putting the One Minute Manager® to Work,* for his wisdom in performance coaching. **Sheldon Bowles,** coauthor of *Raving Fans* and *Gung Ho!,* for his insights into customer service and motivating people. **Wayne Dyer,** for the distinction between ducks and eagles. **Gary Heil** and **Rick Tate,** for their work on *Legendary Service®* and the importance of inverting the traditional hierarchy pyramid, which empowers people to be eagles rather than ducks. **Tim Gallwey,** for his work on the "inner game," and the importance of focusing on process rather than results. **Norman Vincent Peale,** coauthor of *The Power of Ethical Management,* for his important advocacy of positive thinking. **Gordon MacDonald,** for his classic book *Ordering Your Private World,* for the distinction between "called" and "driven" people. **Jan Carlzon,** former chairman of Scandinavian Airline Systems (SAS), for his groundbreaking book *Moments of Truth* and leadership role in service excellence.

Michael O'Connor, coauthor of *Managing by Values,* for his breakthrough work in values in the workplace. **Warren Bennis,** for his continual thoughtful work on leadership. **John C. Carlos** and **Alan Randolph,** coauthors of *Empowerment Takes More Than a Minute* and *The Three Keys to Empowerment,* for their cutting-edge thinking on empowerment. **Bob Schwartz,** for the truth of his book *Diets Don't Work.* **Jesse Stoner** and **Drea Zigarmi,** for their work on the importance of vision. To all the people who have developed Alcoholics Anonymous–like groups to help to overcome people's addictions. **Chuck Colson,** for what he taught us about the ultimate inverted pyramid—dying for your people. **Robert A. Laidlaw,** for his powerful little booklet *The Reason Why* and for his businesslike rationale of why it makes sense to follow Jesus. **Robert Holden,** author of *Happiness NOW,* for his insight into the real meaning of "ego."

Special thanks to **Chuck Heidenreich, Mark Miller, Steve Gottry, John Culea,** and **Jim Despain** for their continual helpful feedback on drafts of the book. Thanks also to the feedback we received from the other folks who attended the Inaugural Center for *FaithWalk* Leadership Conference in January 1999: **Tomas G. Addington, Carlos Arbelaez, Patricia Asp, Denis Beausejour, Sheldon Bowles, Bob Buford, Michael Cardone, John Castle, Dan Cathy, King Crow, David R. Gehr, Ronald D. Glosser, Steve Graves, William A. Jolly, Laurie Beth Jones, Walt Kallestad, Estean Hanson Lenyoun III, Frank Mallinder, David W. Miller, Larry Moody, Tom Muccio, Laura Nash, C. William Pollard, Mike Singletary, Donald G. Soderquist, Reggie Tyler,** and **Dan Webster.**

A special thanks to **Eleanor Terndrup,** for her tireless typing of each of our drafts. Her patience and stick-to-itiveness are world class. Thanks also to **Dottie Hamilt, Kelly DeLuca,** and **Jean Blount** for always being there when we needed them.

We also extend our thanks to our friends and partners at the two publishing houses that jointly released this book—to publisher **Michael Murphy** and sales and marketing manager **Michel Yanson** at William Morrow & Company; and to publisher **Dan Rich,** sales vice president **Doug Gabbert,** and especially to editor **Thomas Womack** at WaterBrook Press. And special thanks to **Margret McBride,** our literary agent and friend, for all her support, feedback, and continual encouragement.

All three of us are blessed with wonderful wives to support us when we should be supported and challenge us when we should be challenged. Thanks **Margie Blanchard, Lynne Hybels,** and **Jane Hodges.** We would also like to acknowledge the memory of **E. P. Hodges,** Phil's dad, who was a constant source of encouragement and early editorial advice prior to this journey back home.

And finally, our three-member consultant team, **The Father, The Son,** and **The Holy Spirit,** for the energy and purpose they have given to our lives on this project. Special thanks for The Word as found in the Scriptures.

List of Scripture Quotations

Page 44: Mark 10:43–44
Page 59: Luke 5:1–5
Page 60: Luke 5:6–7
Page 69: James 4:6
Page 71: Matthew 4:9; 6:1; I Timothy 6:10
Page 74: Matthew 6:33
Page 98: Matthew 28:20
Page 99: Ecclesiastes 4:9–12
Page 116: Matthew 16:26; Romans 12:3
Page 121: Proverbs 29:18
Page 126: Matthew 4:19; John 10:10;
Corinthians 13:13
Page 127: John 8:32; Matthew 28:19–20
Page 142: Mark 9:35; Luke 9:48
Page 143: John 13:12–17
Page 155: Mark 6:8–11
Page 156: Matthew 28:18–20; Matthew 28:20
Page 161: Mark 1:35–37; Mark 1:38
Page 172: Mark 10:43–45
Page 191: Exodus 18:13–23

About the Authors

Ken Blanchard is universally characterized by friends, colleagues, and clients alike as one of the most insightful, powerful, and compassionate men in business today. Few people have impacted the day-to-day management of people and companies more than Ken. He's a prominent, gregarious, sought-after author, speaker, and business consultant.

Ken's impact as a writer is far reaching. His bestselling book *The One Minute Manager®*, coauthored with Spencer Johnson, has sold more than ten million copies worldwide and is still on bestseller lists. This book has been translated into more than twenty-five languages.

Throughout 1996, *The One Minute Manager* appeared on the *Business Week* bestseller list along with three of Ken's other books, *Raving Fans: A Revolutionary Approach to Customer Service* (1993), coauthored with entrepreneur Sheldon Bowles; *Everyone's a Coach* (1995), coauthored with National Football League legendary coach Don Shula; and *Empowerment Takes More Than a Minute* (1995), coauthored with consulting partners John Carlos and Alan Randolph. No other author has had four books on the *Business Week* bestseller list in a single year. *The One Minute Manager, Gung Ho!,* and *Raving Fans* continue to appear on business bestseller lists.

Ken is the chief spiritual officer of the Ken Blanchard Companies, Inc., a full-service, global management training and consulting company that he and his wife, Dr. Marjorie Blanchard, founded in 1979 in San Diego, California. Ken is also a visiting lecturer at his alma mater, Cornell University, where he is a trustee emeritus of the Board of Trustees. Ken also teaches a Master of Science in Executive Leadership degree program jointly sponsored by the University of San Diego and the Ken Blanchard Companies and is cofounder of the Center for *FaithWalk* Leadership.

The Blanchards are proud of the fact that their daughter Debbie, son Scott, and Humberto, Debbie's husband, are also active in their business. They are most proud of their grandchildren, Kurtis and Kyle, sons of Scott and Chris Blanchard.

* * *

From 125 people in 1975 to more than 17,000 today, the ministry of Willow Creek Community Church continues to grow under the leadership of Senior Pastor **Bill Hybels.** Started in a rented movie theater as a means of reaching the nonchurched parents of teenagers in Son City, a youth ministry that Bill cofounded, the church now operates from a 145-acre campus in South Barrington, Illinois, with a staff of over 450.

In addition to his responsibilities at Willow Creek Community Church, Bill is an internationally sought-after speaker, writer, and consultant, and is chairman of the board of the Willow Creek Association, an organization of 4,000 churches worldwide that represents a variety of denominations, locations, and ethnic backgrounds.

The goal of Willow Creek Association is to reach unchurched people and turn them into fully devoted followers of Christ. Services offered by the Willow Creek Association include conferences and workshops, a monthly audiojournal, and an on-line information system, as well as a variety of other communications tools and resources.

Although he intended to follow in the footsteps of his father, a successful businessman, Bill clearly sensed God calling him out of the marketplace and into the ministry. He received a B.A. degree in biblical studies and an honorary Doctorate of Divinity from Trinity College in Deerfield, Illinois. Bill has authored a number of bestselling books, including: *Who You Are When No One's Looking, Too Busy Not to Pray, Honest to God?, Becoming a Contagious Christian, Rediscovering Church, The Story and Vision of Willow Creek Community Church, The God You're Looking For,* and *Making Life Work.*

Bill and his wife, Lynne, reside with their two children, Shauna and Todd, in Barrington, Illinois—except in July and August, when they disappear somewhere on a boat.

* * *

Phil Hodges, for the past thirty years, has held a variety of staff positions in the areas of labor relations and human resource management at Xerox Corporation. As a chief company spokesman at Xerox, Phil negotiated fifty collective bargaining labor agreements for various Xerox manufacturing and distribution organizations.

Phil has extensive experience in interpersonal dispute resolution and is certified by the County of Los Angeles as a mediator. In his most recent assignment with Xerox, Phil played a vital role that resulted in saving a $500 million electronics engineering and manufacturing operation from closure as part of a well-publicized corporate restructuring effort. He was able to forge a unique partnership between local union officials and plant management. The results of this partnership were the upgrade of basic skills competencies, the complete overhaul of job structures and seniority rules, the introduction of performance assessment, operator certification, and gain-sharing programs for a multicultural work force. Eight hundred jobs were saved and record levels of employee and customer satisfaction were achieved.

Phil's long-standing passion for work and family issues, particularly those impacting older workers, is evident. He initiated and implemented Xerox's participation as a founding partner with the County of Los Angeles in a unique Elder Care resource and referral program. He is an active advocate of re-retirement programs and has conducted training for hundreds of Xerox employees and the general public.

Phil has used his leadership and facilitation skills in numerous volunteer activities. Most recent, he completed six years as chairman of his home church, which has a congregation of 3,000 people.

At present Phil is cofounder and the managing director of the Center for *FaithWalk* Leadership, as well as being a consulting partner for the Ken Blanchard Companies.

Phil and his wife, Jane, live in Rancho Palos Verdes, California. They are thrilled that their two children, Phil Jr. and LeeAnne Pinner, live and work nearby with their spouses. Phil and Jane celebrated their thirty-second anniversary this year.

Services Available

Ken Blanchard and Bill Hybels speak to conventions and organizations all over the world. They also have their messages available on audio- and videotapes.

In addition, the Ken Blanchard Companies conduct seminars and in-depth consulting in the areas of customer service, leadership, team building, empowerment for employees to set goals and solve problems, managing by values, and organizational change. Phil Hodges is a consulting partner working in these areas. For further information on the Ken Blanchard Companies or Phil Hodges's activities contact:

The Ken Blanchard Companies
125 State Place
Escondido, CA 92029
(800) 728-6000 or (760) 489-5005
Fax: (760) 489-8407
or visit Ken Blanchard's website at
www.kenblanchardcompanies.com

Ken and Phil are cofounders of the Center for *FaithWalk* Leadership. The center advocates and promotes Jesus Christ and his teachings as a model for leadership. The center accomplishes its goals by training leaders in servant leadership through seminars, counseling sessions, books, and audio- and videotapes. For further information on the Center for *FaithWalk* Leadership contact:

The Center for *FaithWalk* Leadership
125 State Place
Escondido, CA 92029
(800) 728-6000 or (760) 489-5005
Fax: (760) 489-1332

Audiotapes of messages from Willow Creek weekend and midweek services are available individually and on a subscription basis. You may also purchase all Church Leadership Conference and Leadership Summit tapes plus Promiseland videos. To find out more about Bill Hybels's activities contact:

Willow Creek Community Church
67 E. Algonquin Road
S. Barrington, IL 60010
(847) 765-5000
Fax: (847)765-9222

Willow Creek Association is committed to equipping, training, and networking churches for the twenty-first century. Conferences and workshops, a monthly audiojournal, and information websites offer church leaders immediate access to hundreds of Willow Creek drama sketches, message transcripts, creative programming ideas, service order sheets, and the latest information on upcoming events, books, videos, music, and much more! For further information contact:

Willow Creek Association
P.O. Box 3188
Barrington, IL 60011-3188
(847) 765-0070
Or visit Willow Creek's website at
www.willowcreek.org

ALSO AVAILABLE

RAVING FANS!

A Revolutionary Approach to Customer Service

Ken Blanchard and Sheldon Bowles

'Your customers are only satisfied because their expectations are so low and because no one else is doing better ... If you really want a booming business, you have to create Raving Fans.'

Written in the parable style of the bestselling *The One Minute Manager*, it uses a brilliantly simple and charming story to teach how to define a vision, learn what a customer really wants, institute effective systems and make Raving Fan Service a constant feature, not just a passing fad.

By the authors of *Gung Ho!*, *Big Bucks!* and *High Five!*, *Raving Fans!* includes startling new tips and innovative techniques that can help anyone in any workplace to deliver stunning customer service and achieve miraculous bottom-line results.

ALSO AVAILABLE

GUNG HO!

How to Motivate People In Any Organisation

Ken Blanchard and Sheldon Bowles

Increase productivity, profits and your own prosperity! Every day, thousands of uninspired employees trudge to work, often dooming their companies to failure with their lack of motivation.

Gung Ho! outlines foolproof ways to increase productivity by fostering excellent morale in the workplace. Drawing on over 20 years' experience of working with hundreds of corporations, Ken Blanchard and Sheldon Bowles reveal a sure-fire system for boosting employee enthusiasm, energy and performance.

By the authors of *Raving Fans!*, *Big Bucks!* and *High Five!*, and written in the style of the world-beating *One Minute Manager* series, *Gung Ho!* is based on three core ideas to ensure that employees are committed to success and presents a clear gameplan for implementing them.

ALSO AVAILABLE

HIGH FIVE!

The Magic of Working Together

Ken Blanchard and Sheldon Bowles
with Don Carew and Eunice Parisi-Carew

None of us is as smart as all of us, so the bestselling authors of *Raving Fans!* and *Gung Ho!* present the essential tools for turning any group of individuals – from a small unit to a large corporation – into a winning team.

High Five! uses a delightful and charming story to deliver a powerful message on team building and why ten simple words, 'None of us is as smart as all of us,' will work magic for any organisation. With its simple style and easy-to-follow techniques, this book is a must-read for anyone seeking to learn the value and power of teamwork.

'When we wrote *The One Minute Manager* together, one plus one was much greater than two. Now comes *High Five!* Reading this story can motivate us all to be better team players and improve our results.'

From the foreword by Spencer Johnson

ALSO AVAILABLE

BIG BUCKS!

Make Serious Money For You and Your Company

Ken Blanchard and Sheldon Bowles

Big Bucks! offers new and irresistible practical advice to create money and get rich. Like *The One Minute Manager* and *Raving Fans!*, this book uses a business parable to demonstrate how to overcome three challenges – the Test of Joy, the Test of Purpose and the Test of Creativity – to achieve spectacular financial success.

Through a series of easy-to-follow steps and powerful strategies, Blanchard and Bowles show how you can gain wealth and create lasting prosperity. They reveal how, by focusing on concepts like commitment, intensity, purpose and even fun, anyone can build personal wealth and financial security.

Best of all, *Big Bucks!* shows how to accomplish even more valuable achievements by being generous with your time, talents and prosperity, giving significance and meaning to your millions.